£6·00

746·44

EMBROIDERED TEXTILES

D1330344

EMBROIDERED TEXTILES

Traditional Patterns from Five Continents

WITH A WORLDWIDE GUIDE TO IDENTIFICATION

Sheila Paine

With 279 illustrations, 171 in colour

Thames and Hudson

For my children
Denzil ◆ *Rosamund* ◆ *Morwenna* ◆ *Imogen*
who have tolerated so patiently a mother who
always seemed to be thinking about something else
and for Colin

Line Drawings by Imogen Paine
Special photography by Dudley Moss

© 1990 Thames and Hudson Ltd, London
First paperback edition 1995
Reprinted 1997

British Library Cataloguing-in-Publication Data
A catalogue record for this book is available
from the British Library

ISBN 0-500-27823-7

Printed and bound in Singapore by Toppan

Contents

Embroidery is the embellishment of an existing fabric with accessory threads and sometimes with other materials. Such decorative elements as fishskin, teeth, bones, feathers, horn, shells, beetle wings, tassels, beads, coins, buttons, metal and mirror have all at some time or place been used in this way. Most embroidery, however, is straightforward stitchery. The designs are freely drawn, or worked by counting threads, and are applied with a needle, but occasionally with a hook. The thread used is silk, cotton, linen, wool, gold or silver, but also whatever comes to hand, including sometimes even human hair, moosehair, sinew and quills.

A separate technique exists for metal or other precious threads, for non-pliable material such as quills, and for narrow decorative trims, usually cords and braids. These are laid on the fabric and couched down by stitching with another thread, so that none of the decorative material is hidden underneath the cloth.

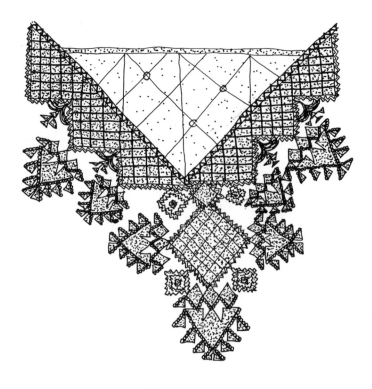

◆◆◆◆◆◆◆◆◆◆◆◆◆◆◆◆◆◆◆◆◆◆

INTRODUCTION: TECHNIQUES AND TRADITIONS

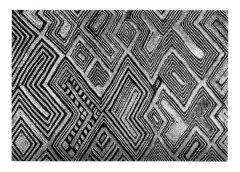

Tattooing decorates and transforms the body. The same patterns are transferred to embroidery, as can be seen, for example, on the textiles of the Kuba people of Zaire.

Opposite: *The name of a pattern usually refers to what it resembles rather than what it represents, as with the 'waterwheels' motif of the dresses of Saraqib in Syria. This recalls the waterwheels of nearby Hama, first described by the fourteenth-century Moroccan traveller Ibn Battúta.*

'Lonely people, delicate people, people without occupation, perhaps, beyond shelling peas, have found embroidery a distraction', declared an article written in the 1920s. It reflected the generally accepted view, which still persists, of embroidery as a pastime for idle ladies – a pastime which, though much modern work can be considered creative art, is more usually relegated by popular opinion to the homely level of a sentimental sampler on the wall, a needlepoint cushion on the fireside armchair, or a linen teacosy worked with crinoline ladies.

These familiar embroideries belong to the domestic tradition of most of Western Europe and of America, where a few elements remain of the original function of embroidery; but here, in the main, the craft has been transformed by fashion, trade and individual choice. Outside the West, on the other hand, embroidery has remained close to its origins.

The primary function of embroidery was to decorate, to embellish textiles already created to meet man's basic needs, and the purpose of such decoration was rooted in ancient beliefs and superstitions. In primitive societies the mysteries of cosmic creation and the human life-cycle were harnessed by mythology: disease and disaster, the causes of which were not understood, were explained by a mythical otherworld of pagan gods, of the evil eye, of good and bad spirits to be praised or appeased. Man could emulate them or protect himself from them by tattooing his body or decorating his clothing with symbols of their powers. Tattooed patterns of peoples as diverse as the Bulgarians, the Tunisians and the Kuba of Zaire are transferred from the body to costume in the form of embroidery. Marco Polo called tattooing 'flesh embroiderie' and indeed embroidery is much more closely related to tattooing than to weaving, felting or knitting. Both employed symbolism expressed in pattern. Both had magical associations.

The shamanistic world of animals and the hunt was one primitive cult at the source of symbolic pattern, as was the earth goddess. Worship of the sun and of trees was also part of the mythology of many pagan societies.

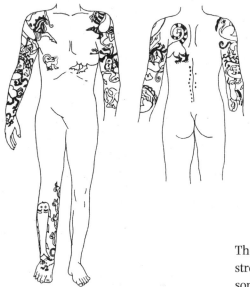

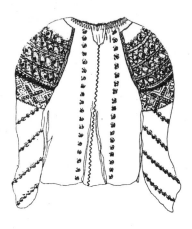

The traditional disposition of embroidery on Rumanian blouses recalls the tattooing of a man found in one of the frozen tombs of Siberia at Pazyryk.

Stylization of pattern was already apparent in the textiles of Pazyryk, dating from about the seventh to the second century BC.

1   Opposite: *Marriage shawl, Siwa oasis, Egypt. The people of Siwa were known as worshippers of the sun god Amon-Ra. The women's marriage robes are embroidered with a sunburst, and their shawls with the solar patterns of spinning wheels, double axes and Maltese crosses. White pearl buttons have been replaced by plastic, but the seven colours of all Siwan embroidery – black, orange, yellow, red, green, blue and white – are adhered to.*

The belief in spirits, both evil and benevolent, dwelling in such places as streams and wells, doors and caves, rocks and trees was universal, and in some societies the power of the evil eye is still feared today.

Most patterns, and the selection of many materials, such as red fabrics and blue beads, derive from the superstitions and symbolism of such cults. The linen towels of Russia are not embroidered with designs of local wildlife – the wolves, wild boars and bears of the region – but with the ancient griffins and peacocks of Iranian art, or with human-headed birds from pre-Christian legend; the blouses of Salamanca in Spain do not depict the domestic animals familiar in everyday life, but the hunted beasts with twisted heads found in palaeolithic rock paintings and in the art of the Scythians, steppeland horsemen who rose into eminence in the seventh century BC. In Japan the appliqué work of the ancient Caucasoid Ainu people, vividly recalling the Chilkat woven blankets of Alaska, is strongly symbolic and a potent protection against the evil eye. It bears no relation to the subtle artistry of commercial Japanese silk and goldwork. Chinese embroidery is generally appreciated for its exquisite workmanship and silken delicacy, but it is riddled with symbolism and played a central role in social hierarchy.

Just as pagan festivals were taken over by formal religions and assimilated into their calendar, so pagan symbolism was often similarly absorbed. Anthropomorphic figures, triangles, pomegranates, carnations and tulips; circles, squares, whorls, swastikas, spirals, 8-pointed stars and birds; diamonds, hooks, dots and waves, zigzags and indentations, columns, plants and crosses, hands and fish – all stem originally from primitive symbolism; and in addition, Buddhism, Hinduism, Islam and Christianity imposed their own symbols from more sophisticated concepts. But it is the common fate of patterns over centuries to be simplified and then abstracted and the symbolism lost. The magic power of horned animals is now concealed in a line of hooks, cockscombs become a row of crests and the sun a simple circle.

continued on page 17

TECHNIQUES AND TRADITIONS

2 *Blouse front, choli, Sind, Pakistan. Patterns derived from sun worship are carved on the desert tombs and are also embroidered on the blouse fronts of Sindhi women.*

3 *Marriage canopy, Kathiawar, Gujarat, India. The lotus is both a Buddhist and a sun symbol. It forms the centre medallion of canopies hung in courtyards at marriages. Other astrological patterns are added, some quilted in blue thread.*

4 *Below: Woman's headdress, kakoshnik Russia. Hair, particularly women's, was universally regarded as magical and covered with a headdress at marriage. In Russia these were handed down from mother to daughter. Pearls are typical of Russian embroidery.*

5 *Opposite: Woman's dress, aba, Kutch, India. The sexual area was often protected by embroidery, in Europe usually by a decorative apron. The Seyhud of Kutch choose an extremely finely worked five-petalled pendant.*

6 *Overleaf: Woman's jacket, Moknine, Tunisia. In the Islamic world the hand of Fatima, khomsa, and the fish are considered powerful talismans against the evil eye. Gold plate, tall, with touches of floss silk on red and green velvet is typical of Tunisian work.*

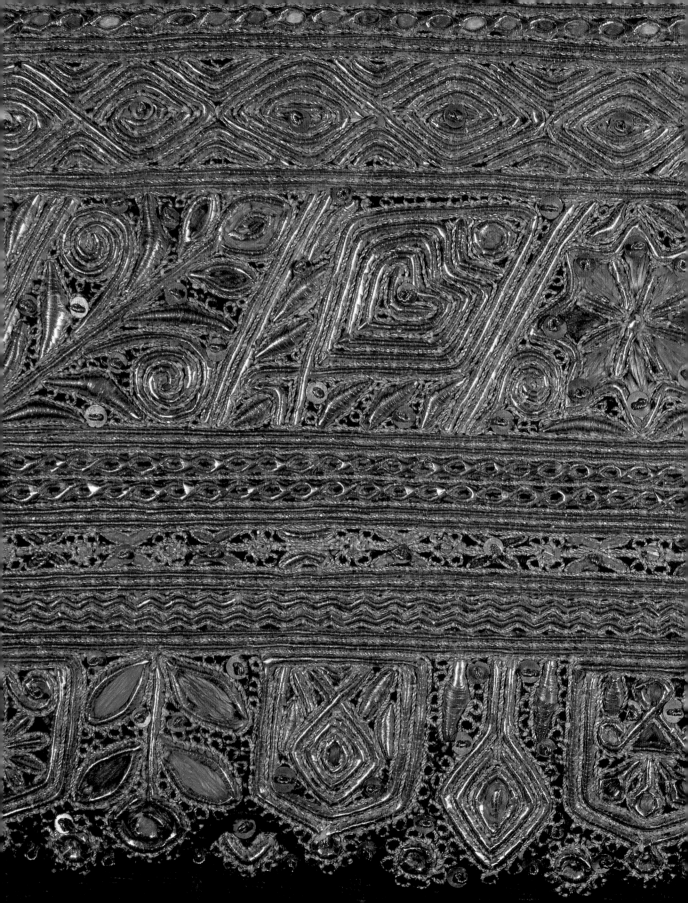

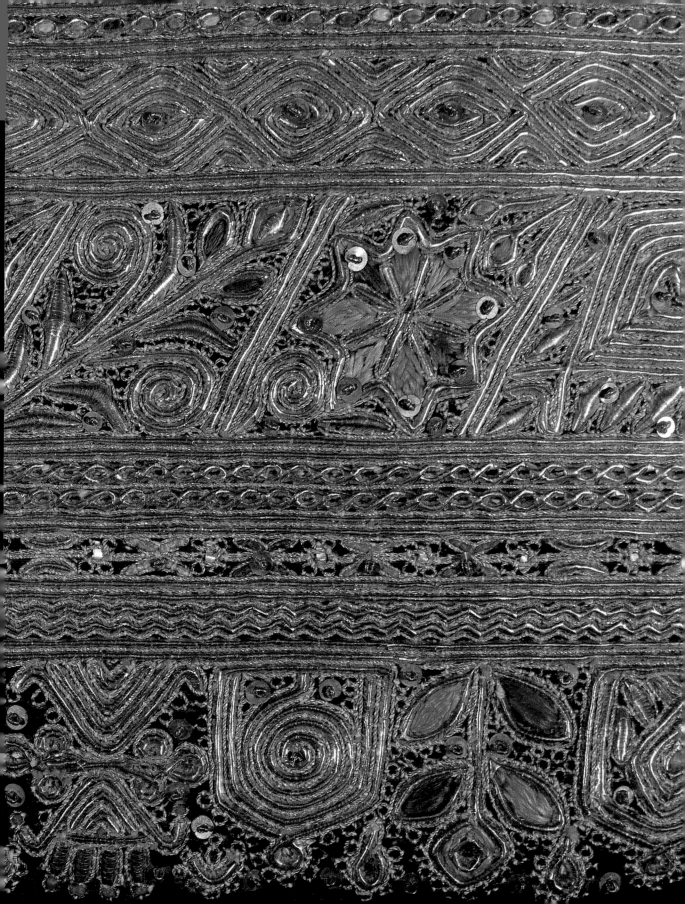

7 *Marriage robe, qmajja, Hammamet, Tunisia. Many ritual embroideries are associated with marriage, among which the shift or robe is the most significant, often also serving as a shroud at death. This robe heavily embroidered with the talismanic fish and hand and various sexual symbols in couched silver thread, areas of* tall, *sequins and coral on alternated bands of silk damask and brocaded silk ribbons.*

8 *Married woman's shawl for 'day of the belt',* tahzim, *El Jem, Tunisia. In North Africa after consummation of the marriage, usually on the seventh day, the ceremony of putting on the belt symbolizes the bride's return to normal life. She wears an enormous woollen shawl, into which the symbolic fish is also woven and which is half henna dyed and half indigo with an embroidered centre panel. This is tied round with a belt in the presence of small boys to ensure she will have sons.*

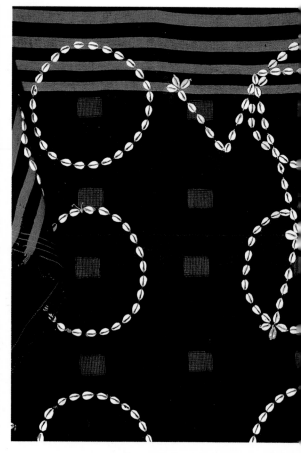

Below: Man's 'killing shawl', Nagaland,
N.E. India. Headhunting was a deeply
symbolic practice to the Naga people, which
even the British during Indian rule were
unable to stamp out. To go on headhunting
expeditions the men wore a 'killing shawl'
decorated with moon motifs in cowrie shells.
Once they had killed, a human figure of more
cowries was added to their shawl.

10   Right: Woman's sarong, tapis, Abung
people, southern Sumatra. The ceremonial
sarongs of the women of southern Sumatra
are worn at all rites of passage and are often
among the textiles buried with the dead.
Embroidery is an unusual technique in the
textiles of Indonesia and may have been
brought by early Chinese traders. Many of
the patterns resemble those on Bronze-Age
gongs.

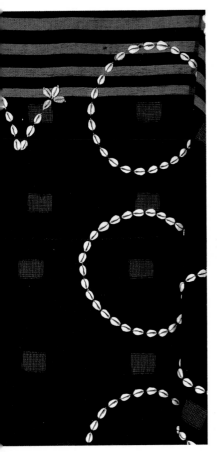

11   Hunter's hat, Baule peoples, Ivory Coast. Stitchery is frequently accompanied b[y] non-textile additions, in the case of this cap by amulets of skin and leopard's claws wrapped in red and indigo fabric, randomly added to the embroidery. The pattern of a lozenge with dot, two crosses and a rectangl[e] are worked in chain stitch on the reverse.

12   Modern panel, England. Varied stitchery, plastified rubbish, leather, frayed hessian. Embroiderers today combine almost anything with stitchery in order to make a personal statement, in this case against litter in hedgerows.

The patterns on the clothing of the Ainu, aboriginal hunters of Japan, have the same totemic quality as the blanket capes of the Chilkat band of the Tlingit North American Indian tribe, living in Alaska. The Ainu garments (as detail top) are of fabric woven from tree fibres, with the patterns appliquéd and embroidered by couching and chain stitch. The Chilkat garments (as detail above) are fingerwoven in goatshair.

The embroideress is normally unaware of their origins: she claims they are just the patterns her mother taught her or that she found in her head. Sometimes, indeed, they are. She also gives them names, such as 'wheels' or 'railway lines', but it is important to remember that these are the names of what the patterns resemble, not what they represent.

This ancient repertoire of pattern is not confined only to embroidery but permeates also all decorative arts, in particular carpets, pottery, wood-carving and what is generally termed 'folk art'; and, most of all, jewelry, which played a magic and religious role as well. There is a certain rigidity in patterns deriving from a cult source, as they are traditionally only used in certain places and in a certain way. Once some freedom in design is apparent, the object is already moving towards the individual interpretation that is an element of personalized art.

Moreover, pattern was not only rooted in belief, but also in the part it played in people's lives and social traditions. The Western concept of embroidery as an individual decorative art or leisure occupation was entirely absent: the item itself, its pattern and colour, were evolved communally. Embroidery therefore came to serve, amongst other things, as a means of identification. On a woman's dress it indicates to an informed observer the village from which she comes, and the colour and disposition of the patterns announce her status as a young girl, married woman or widow. Conventions of decoration establish place in the hierarchy, as in the Chinese court, where embroidered insignia of animals identify the rank of military courtiers and birds that of civil courtiers.

Special occasions are celebrated with embroidery. At all rites of passage, when people are considered most vulnerable to spirits, embroidery plays a symbolic role. In ancient societies death was the most important, more recently, marriage. In Rumania embroideries are hung outside the house of a marriageable girl; in Turkey the fineness of embroidery on the towels a young girl takes to the public baths announces her quality as a prospective daughter-in-law. Dowry and trousseau embroideries are placed on display in most countries as wedding presents are in the West. At childbirth the passage of forty days is marked with protective embroidery for mother and baby, and at death the embroideries worn at marriage serve as a shroud.

If some occasions have spiritual and symbolic potency, so also have certain places. Embroideries are hung where primitive peoples believed spirits to dwell, as at sources of light and water. In Eastern Europe and Morocco they are draped around mirrors and windows, in Germany and Scandinavia near washbasins and doorways. As the hub of the palaeo-lithic home was the hearth, guarded by figurines of the earth goddess, so today's hub, too, is hung with embroideries. This is usually a holy corner with precious icon or perhaps a lurid fairground print of Madonna and Child, augmented with painted plates, with diplomas and photographs and with the family TV. Though the cult object may change over the centuries, the role of embroidery does not.

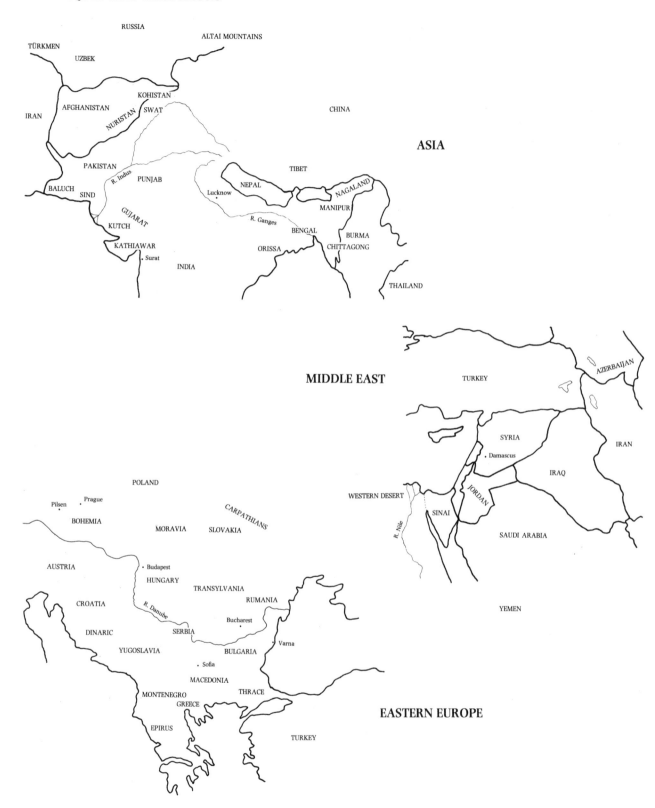

ASIA

MIDDLE EAST

EASTERN EUROPE

◆◆◆◆◆◆◆◆◆◆◆◆◆◆◆◆◆◆◆◆◆◆◆

1
GUIDE TO
IDENTIFICATION

The embroidery of most countries is finite: only certain things are embroidered and only in a certain way. The exception is the modern embroidery of the West, where total freedom of artistic expression allows an embroidery to be identified as the work of a particular person rather than of a society. There is a schism in Western embroidery between the creative work of the individual, and the groundswell of commercially designed canvaswork and kits that give pleasure to thousands of people. All these can be dated with reasonable certainty: no one today embroiders the crinoline ladies of the 1930s nor the cross-sections of green peppers of the 1960s. Western embroidery can thus be assigned to an era but rarely to any particular place.

Embroidery that is closely linked to the customs and beliefs of a society, however, can be very precisely located in place and less easily, less appropriately, located in time. Changes introduced by fashion or the availability of new materials, or else determined by various social factors, were normally minimal, though – as a general guideline – over time, patterns become more abstract, decoration more profuse and workmanship less skilled.

Basic elements to consider when identifying the embroidery of different regions of the world are: the items that are embroidered; their cut and fabric; and the decorating materials, stitches, motifs and styles, especially when one or more of these is unique. There will always be the maverick impossible to locate; but large groups of embroidery do have easily observed characteristics.

THE FAR EAST
China

Chinese embroidery is fine, delicate, professional and the most highly esteemed in the world. It circulates in greater quantity around antique shops, auction houses and art markets than any other, partly because it has now been exported for centuries but also because the imperial city of

Peking was looted during the revolution of 1911. Its high wooden wardrobes were ransacked and shelf upon shelf of the embroidered clothes of the Manchu rulers were sent to collectors and dealers in the West.

Silk is the essence of Chinese embroidery. Silk fabrics – plain, satin, damask or gauze – are worked with floss or twist silk and with threads of gold wrapped round a silk core. The repertoire of stitches is small. Satin stitch, with its variant long and short stitch to provide shading, is by far the most common. Counted thread techniques, such as brick, petit point and cross stitch, are worked only on gauze fabrics. Meticulous rows of small knots – Pekin knot stitch – often fill motifs, and stem and split stitch are used for details. The motifs are outlined and space left between areas of stitchery (a technique known as voiding) and depict flowers, birds, dragons, figures, butterflies and bats, all of which have symbolic significance; other patterns relate to Chinese mythology, as the attributes of the Eight Taoist Immortals. The embroidery is often done on paper or gauze and then applied to the fabric.

The articles embroidered – formal robes and insignia, informal dress, hangings and pictures – were required by court ritual, formalities of costume and demands of trade. Chinese court costume was rigidly controlled and hierarchical; it combined the ancient silk embroidered robe of the indigenous Han Chinese with the close-cut skin coat worn for horse-riding in the steppes by the nomadic warriors, who invaded from Manchuria in 1644, conquered China and imposed a statutory costume that distinguished them as rulers. Best known are the so-called dragon robes, *ch'i-fu*, worn by every official for all but the most formal occasion and decorated with a depiction of the universe, and the informal robes, *ch'ang-fu*, embroidered with symbolic devices, flowers and birds.

These robes are often confused with Japanese kimonos but their cut is distinctive, with a wrapover side-fastening front and slit flared skirt. The sleeves are long and narrow with a mid-length insertion of plain fabric and with horsehoof cuffs, and on women's informal wear they are wide and straight.

Embroidered shoes on raised platform soles were part of Manchu women's costume, and the tiny shoes for bound feet were Han Chinese. Upper-class Han women also wore kilt-like skirts embroidered on the panels and in strips between the pleats. Jacket cuffs of particularly fine embroidery, usually depicting birds and butterflies, or scenes from history and literature, are frequently now sold framed as pictures, as are insignia and skirt panels.

A simple dark coat called a *p'u-fu*, worn over the dragon robe, carries a badge of rank at centre back and front. These insignia are normally square, with the front one split in two for the opening; they depict – in a setting of clouds and sea – an animal, mythical or real, for each of the nine degrees of military rank, and a bird for each of the civil ranks. Purses, and cases for fans, chopsticks, knives and spectacles were worn hanging from a belt.

The cut of the Chinese court robe was based on the early skin garments of the nomadic Manchu rulers. It has a wrapover side fastening and a slit skirt. The dragon robe has sleeves extended by a panel of plain fabric ending in horsehoof cuffs, while the women's informal robes have wide straight sleeves.

These embroidered accessories were often domestic work. Banners for special occasions, exotic theatrical robes, priests' robes and temple hangings were made commercially, or professionally in imperial and monastic workshops.

Professional Chinese embroidery was always exported: by the thirteenth century it was used in Europe for church vestments. From 1578 the Portuguese were allowed to trade from Canton, though until 1840 European 'barbarians' were only allowed to inhabit a wharfside there less than eight hundred yards long and forty yards wide. By the nineteenth century Canton had become a very important centre for export embroidery of hangings, tablecovers, shawls and firescreens. These have a more luxuriant, glossy quality than traditional Chinese, with full-blown flowers and exotic birds. The shawls flooded the Spanish market where they were eventually copied and known as 'Spanish shawls'. Coats and jackets made for the European market were embroidered with the same patterns and techniques as for the Chinese, but in Western cut and rather overloaded in design.

Japan

At a cursory glance Japanese and Chinese embroidery seem very similar: both depict birds and flowers of floss silk and gold thread on a background of silk. Japan, however, did not share the same history, lifestyle and costume as China, and the embroidered articles themselves are quite different.

Most Japanese embroidery is lavished on the kimono. It is easily distinguished from the Chinese robe by its cut of straight strips joined vertically to form both the body and the dangling sleeves, which are of varying length. Exquisitely and precisely tied round the waist is a wide sash, an *obi*, also often embroidered. The same perfection of tying and wrapping extends to gift-giving, and small cloths for presents, *fukusa*, were traditionally embroidered. The recipient was expected to return them.

The classic Japanese home consisted of austere yet aesthetically pleasing areas of space divided by screens. These were usually painted with great artistry but embroidery proved a simple alternative. Hangings made for the home are of sombre colouring and feature landscapes or gracefully posed men and women.

In technique Japanese embroidery also differs from Chinese in that it is normally combined with other types of textile decoration: tie-dye, stencil dye, resist dye, painting, glued gold and silver foil. Embroidery, worked in the same threads and narrow range of stitches as in China, often highlights rather than forms the main pattern. Background fabrics are silks, but also frequently crêpe and some hemp.

Japanese embroidery shows a fine sense of space and of balance: a kimono is often treated as an artist's canvas. Trellis, tartan, geometric repeat and linear patterning in subdued colours – brown, grey and plum – are balanced by curving branches of plum blossom and pine, by reeds and

The Japanese kimono is constructed of straight strips of fabric embroidered and then seamed together. Sleeve shapes vary from short (kosode) to very long hanging (furisode), or are large (osode) or wide (hirosode). The garment is held by a sash, an obi.

grasses, irises and wisteria. A kimono may also be embroidered with a clan symbol, with fans or books in strict repetition, or with a flowing asymmetric landscape of streams, flowers and birds (but in spite of such artistry little heed is paid to whether the design meets exactly at the seams). Where patterns have symbolic meaning – cranes and pine for longevity, the Buddhist treasures – such symbolism is subservient to artistic value.

Korea

The professional embroidery of Korea, *koong-soo*, is close to Chinese but the colours are more daring, blocked rather than shaded, with less gold thread and with outlining rather than voiding. The designs comprise similar flowers, birds and animals, but chequerboard rocks are also an important motif. Items usually embroidered are screens, wedding coats, small accessories, and rank badges of dark blue or green damask. As coats were side-fastening the front rank badge is not split in two as the Chinese is.

The amateur embroidery of women, *min-soo*, decorates the small covers for domestic and ritual use. This bears no relation to the professional tradition of Korea – or for that matter of China or Japan – but has designs of tree and bird spirits emanating from shamanistic beliefs.

Indochina

The embroidery of the tribal groups that straddle the borders of south-west China, Laos, Thailand and Burma exemplifies the immense variety of all tribal and peasant work, where costume differs with each group and village, with the age and status of each woman and with the occasion on which garments are worn. In spite of such diversity, however, certain general characteristics can be singled out.

In this region only garments are embroidered for everyday and for festive use. The fabric is normally indigo or black cotton, sometimes hemp, upon which the embroidery is worked principally in reds and pinks, usually in cross stitch, and patterns are geometric: solid diamonds, 'snowflakes', zigzag, interlaced, serrated, grids in squares, also swastikas, spirals, horns, trees and, especially in appliquéd fabrics, vaguely anthropomorhic and zoomorphic shapes. The costumes are weighed down with decorative appendages: silver discs and tapered pendants, cowries, Job's tear seeds, red seeds, buttons, tassels, pompoms, strips or squares of red flannel and, on singing shawls for funerals, green beetles' wings. Costume varies with each tribe but embroidery can usually be seen on jackets, skirts, leggings, bags, belts, back slings for carrying babies and elaborate headdresses. The women are skilled weavers and produce the clothing for all their family.

Probably best known of Thailand tribal embroidered wear are the swishing full-pleated skirts of the Blue Hmong, with their sections of batik and bands of appliqué and stitchery. The White Hmong concentrate on aprons and on small decorative squares worn at the back neck of their jackets. The showpiece of the Mien are the women 's trousers worked in bands of intricate multicoloured geometric patterning. Jackets, sashes, bags and headdresses of the Akha tribe are decorated with rows of tiny triangles appliquéd in soft colours, outlined with couching, a patterning and technique found also in the embroidery of Ethiopia.

In south-west China bright flowers, dragons, naïve animals, birds and butterflies are added to geometric and hooked designs. A unique group of peasant embroideries from western China comprises household linens and small costume pieces worked in cross stitch in indigo thread on white cotton. Though stylized the motifs are still recognizably Chinese.

Westward into Burma and the hills of north-eastern India and Bangladesh, embroidery on tribal costume is less significant. Simple stitchery supplements brocaded pattern and, for example for the Naga, cowrie shells are a significant ornamentation. Professional embroideries of Burma are heavily sequined padded cloths called *kalaga*, worked mostly in metal threads and depicting mythological Burmese figures.

Oceania

Fine weaving and the decorative techniques of brocading, batik and ikat characterize the textiles of this vast region. Additional decoration sometimes exists as beads, feathers, cowries and other shells. An exception are the ritual skirts, *tapis*, of Lampung, southern Sumatra, on which stripes of ikat are alternated with embroidered ship motifs and touches of tinfoil, mica or spangles. On others primitive anthropomorphic figures are crudely worked in couched metal thread.

In the Philippines European-inspired whitework (white stitching on white fabric) is done on *piña*, a cloth made from the leaf fibres of the pineapple plant.

THE INDIAN SUBCONTINENT

The embroidery tradition of the Indian subcontinent is one of the most richly diverse and masterly in the world. By the sixteenth century Indian floral quilts were already being exported to Europe, embroidered in chain stitch with animals and birds from Gujarat and pictorial ones in wild yellow silk from Bengal.

Indian embroidery, both domestic and professional, is regional and comes almost entirely from northern India. The domestic work of the north west can be recognized by the ubiquitous use of mirror glass, known as *shisha* for Hindus or *abhla* for Muslims, combined with embroidery in which one stitch usually predominates. The most common is open chain, but there are variations with each caste: satin, interlacing, herringbone and chain. The fabric is usually a rough cotton in red, indigo or dark green, or tie-dyed, upon which the embroidery is worked in thick cotton thread with touches of floss silk and sometimes metal; the colours are bright, alternating as black/red, turquoise/orange, and white/indigo. This is a region of cut, as opposed to draped, clothing, where the women made skirts, bare-backed blouses and headcloths for themselves, coats and caps

Chain stitch work of the Kanebi caste of Kutch is in heavy cotton thread of predominantly yellow, pink and white on red cotton.

Chain stitch work of the professional Mochi is in fine silk thread on silk and is done with an ari *hook.*

for their children, and also bags, quilts, wrapping cloths, small covers for food, animal trappings and hangings for festivities and marriage. Patterning is circular or floral, though the Kanebi farming caste also have peacocks, elephants and mangoes as motifs. Wall friezes of the Kathi landowner caste are pictorial, incorporating animals and figures. Cotton appliqué is also a favoured technique, for it uses up old clothing. The Joghi snakecharmer caste makes quilts with straight and fly stitch in subtle colours.

The mirrorwork of the Muslim traders of this region is very fine. Satin dresses are embroidered on the sleeves, over the front bodice and in a star-shaped pendant over the stomach in floral designs of alternating colour. These are worked in minuscule silk buttonhole and chain stitch with tiny pieces of mirror.

Satin skirts with peacocks and flower clusters in chain stitch are the professional work of the Mochi caste, who also undertook commissions for temple hangings. Another, entirely different, type of embroidery from this region are the long narrow sari edgings like ribbons, with Chinese figures or birds. They are either worked in twist thread with cream predominating on a black self-spotted silk, or in pastel floss. Known as *chinai* work, these ribbons, and some clothing, originate in Surat, where many Chinese settled.

From the Punjab come the *phulkari* cloths, made to be worn draped around the body and over the head and to be used as dowry textiles. They are of coarse reddish or indigo cotton embroidered all over in diapered patterning of long darn stitch worked from the back in yellow silk floss, enlivened with touches of puce, purple or green. Those from east Punjab have animal motifs and added *shisha*. From Chamba are found small white cotton cloths called *rumal*, used to cover gifts at weddings and festivals. They are one of the rare pictorial embroideries of India and depict legends and hunting scenes.

In Kashmir the skilled weaving of shawls was emulated more cheaply by embroidery. The same paisley-type patterns, *boteh*, were worked on woollen coats in tiny straight isolated stitches. Today woollen shawls are still embroidered but with simpler motifs. Beige shawls worked with beige couched braid come also from Kashmir, and were fashionable in Europe in the 1850s. Shawls from Delhi are of net or wool worked with floral motifs in satin stitch in vivid floss silks.

The whitework of India known as *chikan*, made by Muslims, is still an important produce of Lucknow. Clothing and tablelinen are worked in chunky stitchery in patterns of trailing stems and small petals combined with larger flowerheads in fine pulledwork.

In north-eastern India Bengal is well known for the covers and wraps for precious objects, known as *kanthas*, which are made out of old white saris. These are quilted in white and embroidered in red and blue running and darning stitch, with symbolic patterns grouped round a central medallion.

The Toda of the Nilgiri hills, ethnically different from the Indian, are the only indigenous embroiderers of southern India.

Embroidery of southern Pakistan includes mirrorwork from Thano Bula Khan and the triangular patterns in satin stitch of the Baluch.

In Orissa umbrellas, banners and canopies are made for religious processions and marriages, with simple bright flowers and animals appliquéd with white chain stitch.

Virtually no indigenous embroidery comes from southern India, except for the work of the Toda tribe and the wandering Banjara. Toda women embroider their draped costume in geometric stripes of red, black and royal blue. The Banjara wear patchwork skirts with waistbands embroidered with solid chevrons and squares in heavy cotton thread. They also embroider bags and belts for their menfolk in the same style.

Commercial goldwork is not localized. Heavy work on velvets or satins was used for elephant trappings and prayer mats, and finer work on silks for saris or tablemats. This usually incorporates some floss silks, purl, spangles or beetles' wings. Patterns are floral or of Mughal inspiration.

In what is now Pakistan the tradition of north-western India – domestic work using *shisha* – continues into Sind. Here hangings and coverings are distinguished by circles worked in a radiating stitch, usually in shades of red silk. Further west, the cotton dresses of the Baluch have very fine embroidery on the front bodice and all edges. Geometric patterning, especially triangles, are worked in alternating colouring. Underarm gussets are usually in a bright contrasting colour, a tradition that spreads across north-west India and Central Asia. The silk dresses of the Baluch have fine multicoloured embroidery, including interlacing, on the shoulder, front bodice, edges and on a central long front pouch, a *pudo*. Northward in Swat clothing and cushions are in black cotton, or occasionally white, embroidered with medallions in shocking pink silk.

CENTRAL ASIA

The embroidery of the Central Asian steppelands is tribal. Textiles – carpets, felts and to a lesser extent embroideries – were always highly prized articles in a nomadic lifestyle.

Best known are the dowry hangings and bedspreads of the Uzbek, known as *suzanis* (from the Persian and Tadjik word for 'needle'). Made of strips of bleached cotton or linen they are covered with flowers embroidered mainly with pinkish red silk. Leaves and stems divide the field and the flowers range from naturalistic sprays on those from around Nurata in the west, through large isolated floral heads, to stylized solar symbols from Pskent in the east. From the mid-nineteenth century they were made for sale and are still favoured collectors' pieces.

Innumerable small articles are embroidered: tent hangings of every description, purses, bags, small cloths, prayer mats, clothing, covers for bicycle saddles, telephones and guns, and especially caps in a great variety of patterns for men and children. Fabrics are silks, mainly red or purple, and red or black cotton. Patterned cotton fabric from Russia, India and England, either block printed or resist dyed, mainly with floral or small repeat designs, is commonly used to line embroidery throughout this area and in northern India, Russia, the Middle East and the Balkans.

Pattern and stitch vary with tribe or region. The Uzbeks favour dense geometric patterns in cross stitch, but the Lakai sub-group have more freewheeling circles and hooks in varied stitches. The Türkmen use an interlaced stitch, *kesdi*, that gives a filled band with a ridge each side. The Hazara, a Mongol minority settled in central Afghanistan, work squiggly patterns in monochrome chain stitch, usually red or orange, edged with blue beads. The tribal peoples of Kohistan embroider patterns of serrated diamond and zigzags in petit point, cross stitch and brick stitch with white bead edging, and in Kandahar fine pulledwork is combined with white quilting and satin stitch in white floss silk.

Clothing is equally varied. The Türkmen women wore cloaks, called *chyrpy*, with vestigial sleeves in dark green or indigo silk for young girls, yellow for married women and white for old. They are decorated with tulips, versions of the tree of life and hooked carpet motifs. Red silk dresses and coats are embroidered in the same style. Dresses from Afghanistan are familiar in the West from their popularity in the 1960s. Full skirts are gathered to a high waist with embroidered square front bodice, and extra long sleeves end in embroidered cuffs. This is the north-western extent of the use of *shisha* in embroidery. The wedding dresses of Kohistan are cut with hundreds of godets, like the skirts of Greek soldiers, and are embroidered with red floss silk in dense geometric pattern and circles, with added white beads and buttons.

In the eastern reaches of Central Asia Chinese-style robes with wide cut sleeves are embroidered in chain stitch with patterns in medallions.

Embroidery of the tribal peoples, living in the remote mountain valleys of Afghanistan and northern Pakistan, features red stitchery in geometric patterns edged with white beads and with added white buttons.

THE MIDDLE EAST
Iran

Most embroidery is imitative of the country's superlative carpets, velvets and brocades, with the garden as the major source of inspiration. Iran is unique among Islamic countries in also having textiles with figurative motifs.

The most familiar embroideries from Iran, popular in Europe since the nineteenth century and frequently cut up into bags, cushions and upholstery fragments, are called 'gilets persans', a euphemism for women's trouser legs, and consist of solid diagonal bands of flower heads in silk twist mainly in pinks and beiges. From Resht in the north come hangings and prayer mats of patchwork, or appliqué of flannel or felt, depicting vases, bouquets of flowers, or trees with birds. Decorative stitchery accentuates all the joins.

Couched goldwork flowers with fillings of floss silk decorated court cushions, rugs and covers. Whitework cloths display a wide variety of techniques used in one piece, each area separated by needleweaving.

Iraq

Embroidery centres on the northern village of Qaracoche where Christian women wore shawls and dresses embroidered with a cross and other symbols roughly stitched in bright colours.

The Gulf States

Urban embroidery is mainly goldwork on caftans and caps, much of it imported from India. Small caps for men are common throughout the Islamic world; many are quilted with superimposed coloured stitchery, or are in eyelet work, such as those from Oman.

Dresses of the desert tribes of Saudi Arabia are of black cotton cut wide with deep sleeves and with appliquéd squares of fabric over the shoulders and hem, decorated with minimal embroidery.

Turkey

The quality of most Turkish embroidery is extremely fine. The small domestic articles and dress accessories – napkins, towels, sashes – are made of a white to pale beige slightly crinkly cotton, and their floral motifs, with pink and green as favourite colours combined with goldwork, are worked by women. Outlining is a typical feature of Turkish embroidery, and the motifs – of individual flower sprays, or a flowerhead below a serrated curved leaf or hyacinth stem – are normally repeated two, three or four times. Apart from flowers, the symbolic kiosk appears, and on napkins occasionally fruit, but never animals or figures. Decorative edges, usually of alternating colours or small lace flowers called *oya*, worked with a needle or crochet hook, are another distinctive feature.

Turkish embroidery can be divided specifically by technique. On these small domestic pieces stitches are normally reversible, with a few exceptions, such as trouser legs which have vertical bands of non-reversible floral embroidery divided by needleweaving. Professional work includes appliqué (mainly for court items) and tamboured chain stitch on silk for hangings and the barbers' aprons in vogue in the eighteenth

The flowerhead encircled by a curving leaf, known as the saz motif, is typical of Turkish embroidery and spread throughout the Ottoman empire.

century. Diagonal darning imitating a twill weave was used in hangings of the sixteenth to eighteenth centuries and straight darning on fine wrapping cloths, headscarves and turban covers of the seventeenth and eighteenth centuries. Motifs of artichokes and tulips, of flowers enclosing smaller unworked floral patterns and the symbolic three balls and wavy lines (çintemani) are usually in main colours of red and blue. Baroque flower designs cover velvet dresses worn for marriages.

Goldwork, *dival*, was an important Turkish technique, most commonly worked over card; the thread is couched in whirls and *boteh* on jackets, coats and waistcoats made all over the Ottoman empire. Almost all Turkish patterns and techniques are found throughout the countries they subjugated: the same pomegranate design decorates Hungarian leather jackets and Moroccan mirrorcloths.

THE BIBLICAL LANDS

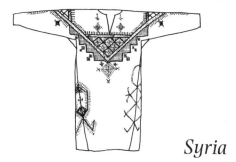

Embroidery from northern Syria to the Bedouin of eastern Egypt features mostly on long dresses of indigo or black cotton with straight or winged sleeves, although linen, rayon, undyed or striped fabrics are also used. Their patterns are geometric or of a stylized floral design, mainly worked in counted thread, especially cross stitch, in silk. The dresses were worn with ornate headgear and jewelry – a simplified version is in fact still worn as a political statement identifying the Palestinian Arab woman throughout the region.

Syria

The disposition of embroidery on Syrian dresses is in V-shapes at neck and sides of skirt, and on indoor dresses on the centre skirt front and winged sleeves.

Embroidery on Syrian dresses extends mainly in a V-shape over front and back neck and shoulders like a cape, on the skirt sides in asymmetric form and on the sleeves. Patches of fabric, either striped silk from Aleppo or the printed cotton of Central Asia, are appliquéd inside the neck and hem, defined on the outside by red stitchery. Carnations stylized into hexagons are the most common motif. There are regional differences, particularly around Damascus where white or sometimes red indoor dresses are embroidered on the winged sleeves and in an inverted V on the skirt front with small flowers and risers of cypress trees, worked in outline in pink and green. Cloths, purses and mirror-hangings were also embroidered and some coats and skirts.

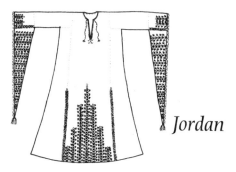

Jordan

In southern Syria, northern Palestine and northern Jordan dresses are cut loose and wide. Inserted strips of blue or white fabric and bands of white embroidery leaving the pattern in reserve are edged with satin or fishbone stitchery. Elsewhere there is minimal embroidery to accentuate edges and seams in bright alternating colours, again in satin or fishbone stitch.

Palestine

This is the most complex area of these parts, with strong regional differences. The fabrics which bear Palestinian embroidery are varied: indigo, black, undyed or striped cotton, or sometimes linen or silk. In

On Palestinian dresses the embroidery is usually in a square neck placket and in blocks on the sleeves and skirt.

The positioning and patterns of embroidery on the wing-sleeved dresses of the Bedouin of Sinai emulate those of Palestinian village women.

general, embroidery is stitched on a square front chest panel – often enclosing a V-shape –, on the sleeves and around the skirt hem to varying degrees of depth and with special emphasis on the back; headveils and cushions are also embroidered. The disposition is of rigid vertical blocks of geometric pattern mainly in cross stitch in reddish brown silks.

The embroidery of Bethlehem is of circles and flowers of couched threads enclosing bright floss silks. Touches of this technique are in evidence on dresses of other areas, and also chevrons and patches of appliquéd cottons or striped silks, usually accentuating edges. These often help identify Palestinian embroidery. Dresses from Jerusalem are in Bethlehem style but on white cotton tamboured with yellow silk, usually imported from Syria. In the Gaza area the chest panel is a simple V-shape and the indigo fabric has a purple or green striped edge. In the north, coats were embroidered until the mid-nineteenth century.

Egypt

Bedouin dresses of the eastern desert continue in the Palestinian style but with much cruder work. Bright geometric patterns, with some stylized birds and figures, are worked horizontally in cotton thread in a deep level band all round the skirt and on the winged sleeves. In the western desert the oasis towns have wide loose black or white dresses ornamented by linear embroidery and scores of buttons in a sunburst from the front neck placket. Best known of Egyptian embroideries are the appliqué panels copying tomb wall-paintings, still made by men in the Cairo markets, and the net scarves of Azute with geometric patterns of silver.

Yemen

Yemeni embroidery is found mainly on women's dress, though the belts in which the men wear their curved daggers are decorated with the traditional pattern of a cursive line in gold thread. The garments vary in style from region to region.

In the southern mountains dresses are embroidered in solid lines in a deep V at the front neck and over almost the entire dress, in white cotton thread with touches of red, green and yellow. Dresses of the coastal plain are of black cotton, cut narrow in Bayt-al-Faqih and wide in Bajil, appliquéd in grid patterns in white and silver braid, with areas of silver plate and red and green cotton embroidery.

In Sada'a in the north, wide wedding dresses of yellow striped Aleppo silk have triangles appliquéd over the breasts and small vertical lines of silver embroidery, culminating in a white button and a tassel. Bright patchwork squares are hidden under the cuff of the deep sleeves. Around Sana'a, capital of northern Yemen, short indigo dresses are decorated with brass sequins, augmented by red and white cotton linear embroidery. Others are covered with complex patterns in chain and running stitch in evenly balanced red, green, yellow and white cotton and silver thread. Many dress patterns are the same as those of the adobe buildings of Yemeni towns and villages. Urban dresses, worn under black shrouds, are often adorned with silver amulets and coins. Trousers embroidered at the cuff with couched silver thread in bands of diamonds and circles were Jewish work.

The Jewish population of Sharaf in the north west, now all resettled in Israel, embroidered indigo dresses with deep zigzag patterning on the front chest. Two symmetric panels are worked each side of the front neck placket, and two asymmetric below, especially over the left pocket. The patterns have a close affinity with the Hausa robes of Nigeria.

AFRICA SOUTH OF THE SAHARA

In Islamic West Africa there is a strong tradition of skilled strip weaving, tie-dye, indigo dyeing and – in some areas such as Nigeria, Liberia and Cameroon – embroidery, especially on men's robes. These are cut extremely wide with no separate sleeves and are embroidered in bold asymmetric patterning of interlacing, spirals, squares, triangles and circles at the neck and in a deep area over the left breast where the pocket is placed. Those of the Hausa of Nigeria are best known, having distinctive long triangles worked in monochrome cotton thread, mainly in open chain, diagonal satin and eyelet stitch. The excessively wide trousers worn under them are embroidered in brightly coloured wools in entirely different curvilinear patterning and chequer effects, and the women's draped cloths are worked in the same style.

Women's robes of the Bornu of Nigeria and the Kotoko of Chad are cut with straight deep sleeves and have a deep oval of zigzag patterning surrounded by interlacing at the neck, with the rest of the robe covered with grid patterns and circles, claimed to symbolize the local princely settlement and the mythology of his power.

In non-Islamic Africa beadwork is the most common decorative technique but there is some appliqué, especially on ceremonial items such as the banners of the Fon of Dahomey, where religious, hunting and war scenes are depicted with naïve animals and figures. The Kuba of Zaire appliqué women's skirts with raffia and embroider cut-pile raffia funeral cloths in sophisticated maze-like patterns of all-over interconnecting lines and squares, in natural beiges and browns.

THE MAGHREB
Morocco

The indigenous Berbers of Morocco are weavers; refugees from Andalucia brought embroidery to the Moroccan cities, each of which has its own individual style.

Fez is the most prolific. Cushions and covers of poor cotton are worked with monochrome floss silk, usually red, in a stepped running stitch which is reversible. Patterns are disciplined geometric borders flanked by small stylized floral risers. Embroideries of the old pirates' haunt of Salé are in the same stitch as those of Fez but loosely worked, giving a bouclé effect. Newer work is in long-armed cross stitch and not reversible. Patterns are stylized plant motifs. The embroidery of neighbouring Rabat is drawn and not counted. Curtains of fine white cotton, often tamboured in white, are worked with floral motifs in satin stitch in brilliantly coloured floss silks.

In the royal city of Meknès scarves and cloths in fine etamine are edged with massed floral patterning and scattered with small flowers, worked in stepped running stitch in polychrome silks.

Borders in Italian Renaissance style from the small port of Azemmour resemble those of Sicily, Parga in Greece and Avila in Spain. The background is filled with long-armed cross stitch in red, or occasionally blue, floss silk. Motifs of a plant or figure flanked by birds are outlined in black or beige, with small details in the same colour.

Tetouan was settled after the reconquest of Andalucia and embroidered mirror hangings and cushions were made for display at marriage in the European tradition, not for Arab-style use on the floor. Fine quality cotton is worked with soft coloured silks in drawn floral motifs.

Algeria

Fine cotton curtains, scarves and bonnets were made in Algiers in the seventeenth and eighteenth centuries in the contemporary Turkish style of darning, but with greater stylization. Large floral-derived motifs in red and blue silk are contrasted with small flowers in pastels and some goldwork.

Tunisia

Goldwork on clothing is the principal embroidery of Tunisia, particularly on coifs and marriage robes, which were often made of strips of silk ribbon, and on waistcoats with heavy gold epaulettes. The work is distinguished by the use of flat metal plate worked over thick cotton, which looks like gilded leather, with touches of bright floss silk. The embroidery is normally on silk or velvet, particularly red and green together, and the motifs are talismanic.

The Greek Islands

While mainland Greek embroidery, excepting that from the prosperous mountainous Turkish province of Epirus, is in the main Balkan tradition, the work from the islands – footholds for all who plied the eastern Mediterranean between Asia, Europe and North Africa – is a hybrid, influenced by both Venice and Turkey. Not all island peoples embroidered, and it is impossible to say why some did not. The most important embroideries are the bed-tents or hangings (depending on the architecture of the island), with costume of lesser significance.

Most prolific was the island of Naxos. Bedspreads and wall-hangings are of red silk, shaded by a change in direction of stitch, in all-over repeat motifs of four leaves forming a circle around a central pattern, with areas in reserve. The bed-tents of Rhodes are in red and green thick floss in long-armed cross stitch, the motif on the field derived from a flower vase and edged with a repeat pattern of slanting leaves. Birds figure at the top of the

31

The pictorial embroideries of Skyros include motifs, half animal or bird, holding branches in their hands, as does the goddess depicted on the great felt of Pazyryk.

door opening. The bed-tents of Kos are finer, in pattern darning with more varied pictorial motifs – birds, ships, figures – over the door. Many bedlinens are difficult to ascribe to a precise island. Distinct, however, are the pictorial designs of Skyros, mainly of goddesses and ships, and the marriage processions on the Turkish-style hangings and cushions of Epirus and the Ionian islands.

A striking feature of Greek island embroidery is that the colour range is limited to red, green and blue with yellow and beige, the tonal quality varying with the island. Mostly it is soft and muted, but bright and clear in Crete and with added pastel shades in Skyros. Work is either counted thread or freely drawn.

Costume is of varied cut and materials. Italian influence is visible in fine drawn threadwork and Turkish in goldwork, needleweaving and *oya* edgings known as *bibíla*. Such edgings in the islands and in Epirus contrast with tassels and fringes in Balkan tradition in the rest of the mainland. Velvets and silks occur as frequently as cottons and linens. Dresses are shifts with sleeves or simple straight petticoats gathered into a band above the bust. Those of Skopelos are black with repeat motifs of green and yellow vases with red flowers and those of Crete have a narrow band of repeat pattern in scrolls, topped by a wide frieze of flowing design based on a recurring motif of flower vases linked by patterns of flowers and mermaids. They show a strong affinity with the Renaissance designs in Italian pattern books.

EASTERN EUROPE

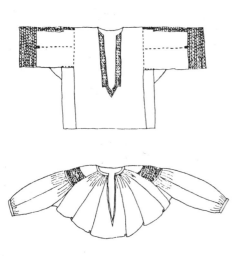

The cut of the linen clothing of Eastern Europe is either in straight sections (Dinaric) or gathered into the neck (Pannonian). Both use every scrap of precious linen fabric.

The embroidery of Eastern Europe is on peasant costume of linen and wool, and on bedlinens for display at marriage, childbirth and death. There is immense diversity from village to village and the twentieth-century political boundaries are largely irrelevant.

Linen blouses and shifts, worked in counted thread, are of two types of cut – Dinaric (cut straight with a fold at the shoulder, slit front placket, and straight sleeves with underarm gusset) and Pannonian (having the sleeve and body gathered together into a narrow neckband, with slit front placket and underarm gusset. The sleeves are drawn into a frilled or straight cuff and sometimes have a separate gathered shoulder seam). Purchased white cotton later replaced hard-won home-produced linen, but the cut of the garments, which wasted not a square inch of precious fabric, remained unchanged. Patterns are usually geometric, though Turkish-influenced floral motifs extend as far west as Hungary, and aprons and headscarves are usually decorated with floral designs in silk. Linen shirts for men are mostly worked in drawn threadwork techniques.

Jackets and coats of wool are boldly decorated with freely drawn archaic patterns, and those of sheepskin have floral motifs. Everywhere in the Balkans jackets and coats of Turkish-style goldwork were professionally made.

continued on page 57

3   Panel from a woman's kilt, China. The
rge flower is in Pekin knot stitch in silk
vist and the rest of the embroidery in satin
itch with voiding, worked in floss silks on
tin. Wraparound kilts derive from the
uble apron worn by the nomadic Manchu
fore they conquered China. They have two
nbroidered panels front and back and some
otifs in a vertical line in each section of the
irt.

4   Woman's summer jacket, China.
ounted thread technique of petit point and
rick stitch; faces, hair and hands in satin
itch. Silk thread on silk gauze. This jacket
picts scenes from the opera 'The West
hamber', a boy-meets-girl love story. In
is medallion the boy is dreaming of the girl
s he writes to her. Narrative scenes are rare
Chinese embroidery.

5   Court insignia, mandarin duck of a
eventh-degree civil official, China. Couched
old thread with silk on silk fabric.
mbroidered badges on the plain coats of
hinese court officials marked their rank by
irds for civil and animals for military.

16 Hanging, Canton, China. Satin stitch in
*silk twist and floss on silk. The ordered
disposition of Chinese embroidery is absent
from articles made for export, which tend to
be luxuriant and free-flowing in style, though
still with symbolic meaning. In this hanging,
phoenixes, symbol of the empress, are
perched on boughs surrounded by
chrysanthemums, symbol of autumn.*

17 Kimono, Japan. Birds in satin and long
*and short stitch are worked in floss silk on to
a design already resist dyed into the crêpe
fabric with a rice paste. Couched gold flowers
and leaves are added. The entire kimono is a
landscape of resist-dyed waterfalls, rivers and
bushes, with embroidered flowers and birds.
This mixture of techniques would not be
found in Chinese embroidery.*

18 Woman's hood, Akha tribe, Thailand.
*Appliquéd triangles of cotton fabric edged
with couched thread and with satin stitch,
fishbone and back stitch patterns, all in
alternating colours. Cotton thread, additional
white buttons and beads on indigo cotton.
Other hill tribes of Thailand embroider in a
different style, but predominantly on indigo
in cross stitch, mainly in pinks.*

19 Cloth, kalaga, Burma. Padded and
*appliquéd dancing figure with couched metal
threads, sequins and beads. Such cloths, often
depicting figures from Buddhist mythology,
hung in temples or on bullock carts at
festivals.*

Woman's sarong, tapis, Kauer people, ~~[sou]~~thern Sumatra. Striped weave with bands ~~[of p]~~attern embroidered in couched gold and ~~[seq]~~uins. Designs varied with the tribe and are ~~[of c]~~ouched metal in fluid shapes, or of ships ~~[car]~~rying people and trees in cream, brown ~~[and]~~ blue silks, alternated with bands of ikat. ~~[Sm]~~all pieces of mica or mirror, cermuk, are ~~[nor]~~mally added.

~~[TH]~~E INDIAN SUBCONTINENT

Sari edging of chinai work, Surat, ~~[Ind]~~ia. Satin stitch in twist silk with floss for ~~[fac]~~es and hands on silk satin. These can also ~~[be]~~ worked in floss silk and the fabric can be a ~~[fin]~~e black silk woven with an allover spot ~~[des]~~ign. Birds are a common motif.

Phulkari, East Punjab, India. Back ~~[stit]~~ch and darning in floss silk on brick red, ~~[han]~~d-woven cotton, khaddar. While the ~~[phu]~~lkaris of West Punjab are covered by ~~[geo]~~metric patterning, those of East Punjab ~~[are]~~ worked with figures and animals. often ~~[wit]~~h shisha. Khaddar can also be indigo.

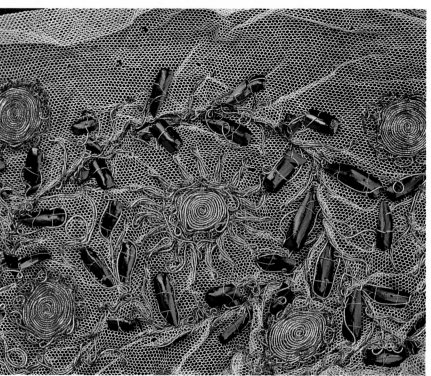

23   Motif at back neck of coat, Kashmir, India. Exceptionally fine straight and chain stitch in silk thread on wool. Kashmiri shawls were similarly embroidered, imitating cheaply the woven ones. The curving motif known as boteh is a hallmark of Kashmiri work.

24   Man's coat, angarkha, Lucknow, India. Chikan work. Characteristic of the chikan work of Lucknow are the large flowerheads of pulledwork with smaller flowers. These are usually chunky or, when worked in shadow stitch as here, flatter textured.

25   Border of dress, India. Couched gold thread and beetles' wings on net. Beetles' wings were used extensively in Indian embroidery, usually combined with metal threads on muslin or net.

26   Hanging, Sind, Pakistan. Radiating stitch with ridged edge, floss silk thread on silk. This stitch is typical of northern Sind and is the use of shades of pink and red.

7 Woman's shift, Swat, Pakistan. Floss
~~silk~~ satin stitch on cotton, silver amulets.
~~Shocking~~ pink is typical of Swat work.

CENTRAL ASIA

8 Suzani, Uzbekistan, Central Asia. Silk
~~on~~ silk, with both the laid and couching
~~thread~~ the same. In Bokhara the tying stitch
~~is~~ small and in Roumanian long.

9 Purse, Hazara, Afghanistan. Silk chain
~~st~~itch on cotton, blue and white beads.

10 Saddle cover, Ghazni, Afghanistan.
~~Co~~uched silver threads, shisha, open chain.

11 Tekke Türkmen woman's cloak, chyrpy,
~~T~~urkmenistan. Interlaced stitch kesdi, in
~~t~~wist silk on silk. The main motif is the tulip.

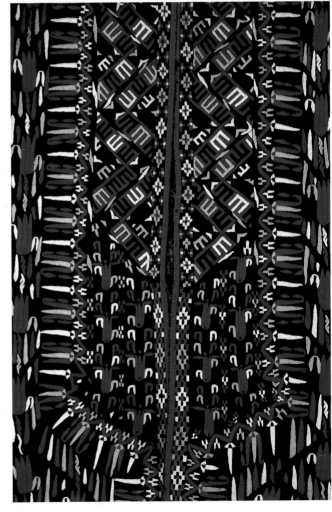

32 Woman's trouser legs, nakshe,
Azerbaijan, Iran. Dense cross stitch and petit
point in diagonal lines, silk twist on cotton.
The embroidery of Persia, like the much more
important carpets and brocades, celebrated
the garden, though it is one of the few in the
Islamic world also to depict figures.

33 Napkin border, Turkey. Repeat floral
motif in reversible stitchery of Turkish stitch
similar to stem stitch, in shades of green and
pink, combined with metal threads on fine
cotton fabric. Outlining, gözeme, is another
frequent technique of Turkish embroidery, as
is the netted stitch musabak.

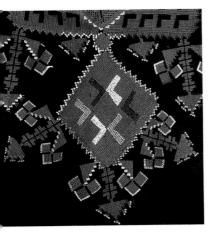

THE BIBLICAL LANDS

34 Woman's dress front, Saraqib, Syria. Cotton thread on black cotton sateen. The deep V-shaped embroidery of the front of shifts of this village always finishes in a pendant called 'waterwheels'. The work is done by eye and not counted thread and is consequently never geometrically accurate.

35 Bedouin dress of Sinai desert, Palestine. Cross stitch in blue cotton on black cotton fabric. Skirt embroidery is predominantly blue for unmarried girls and widows and red for married women. Unlike Palestinian village embroidery Bedouin work often has small birds and anthropomorphic shapes as part of the pattern.

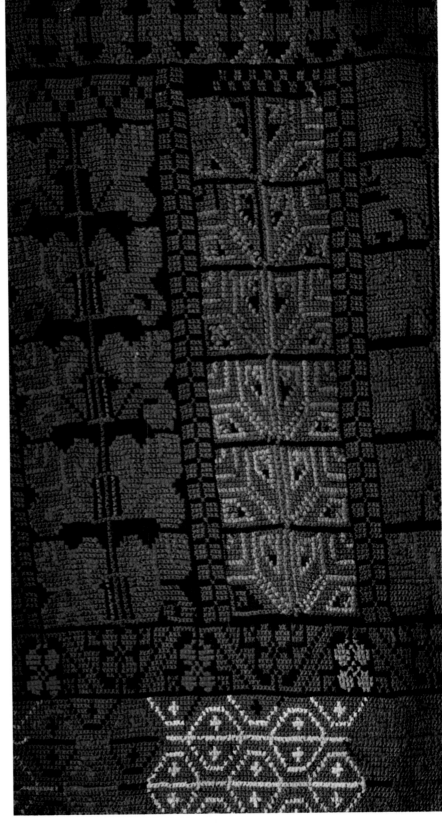

36 Woman's dress, Bayt al-Faqih, Tihama coastal plain, Yemen. Shaped dress decorated with appliquéd white and silver braid and sections in red and green cotton and silver plate at neck, cuffs and hips. Black cotton fabric with acrylic print insertion. The dresses of nearby Bajil are the same but in a loose wide cut.

AFRICA SOUTH OF THE SAHARA

37 Woman's dress, Logone Birni, Chad, Africa. Satin, chain and blanket stitch in floss silk on cotton. The dress is knee-length, cut wide with side skirt insertions and deep straight short sleeves. The patterns are believed to symbolize myths of the origins of the royal town and the fishing nets that are the source of its wealth.

38 Patchwork banner of military company, Fanti people, Ghana, West Africa. Cotton fabric joined with run and fell seams, with appliqué and chain stitch embroidery in cotton. Appliqué is a common African technique, while patchwork was also used for quilted horse armour by the Fulani of northern Cameroon.

39 Men's trousers, Hausa people, Nigeria, West Africa. Chain stitch and couching in wool on fabric of joined strips of indigo cotton. The trousers are of extremely wide cut. The anthropomorphic figure is reminiscent of the earth goddess. Hausa womens' robes, but not mens', are often embroidered with similar patterns and technique.

40 Man's robe, West Africa (precise origin not known). Chain stitch and buttonhole in red, pale blue and cream cotton on beige cotton with red felt outlining neck. The snake is attacking a toad. Other motifs include an anthropomorphic figure with raised arms, two more snakes and further linear geometric patterns. The robe is of a very wide cut.

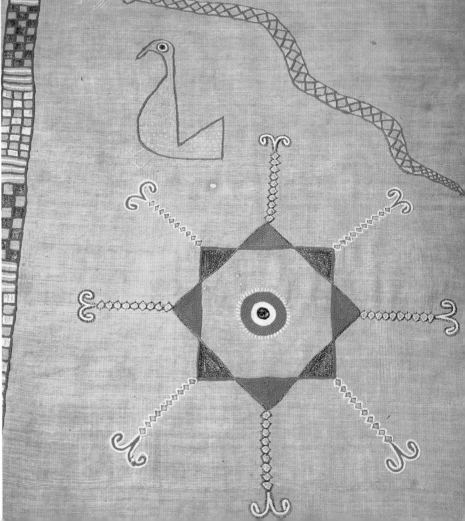

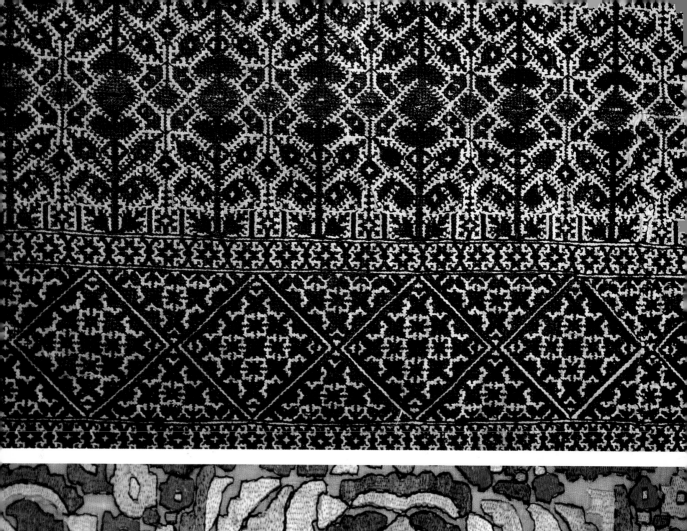

HE MAGHREB

1 *Cushion cover, Fez, Morocco.*
eversible stepped running stitch point de
ait *in floss silk on cotton. This stitch*
orked in monochrome – usually red – is
aracteristic of Fez. Patterns are a triple
rder of diamond motifs with small floral
sers at one edge and large at the other.

2 *Mirror hanging, Tetouan, Morocco.*
eversible brick and satin stitch with black
utlining, needleweaving at edge. Floss silk
n fine cotton. These cloths were hung over a
irror opposite the marital bed for forty days
ter the wedding.

3 *Woman's bonnet,* benîqa, *Algiers.*
yelet stitch in floss silk, couched metal
reads on cotton. The design is Turkish-
fluenced. These bonnets were worn at the
ammam with the lappets wound round the
air as a towel.

4 *Marriage undershift, Moknine, Tunisia.*
all, silk details and floss silk tassels, on
otton. The black motifs are the same as
ose tattooed on the woman, while the
gures represent the fertility goddess.

THE GREEK ISLANDS

45 *Fragment, Rhodes, Greek Islands. Cross stitch in floss silk on cotton. Both the motif, known as glastra vase, and the technique are characteristic of the bed-tents, valances and cushions of Rhodes. A raised chunky effect is achieved by using very thick loosely twisted silk in a slack cross stitch, normally alternating in red and green and with a border of slanting leaves in a yellow shade.*

EASTERN EUROPE

46 *Front of woman's shift, Macedonia, northern Greece/southern Yugoslavia. Cross stitch in wool on linen. Dense geometric patterns, especially based on the diamond, with hooked edges and worked in wool in dark colours or in red, are typical of much of the Balkans.*

47 *Hem of woman's shift, Attica, Greece. Petit point in floss silk on cotton. The shift hems of Attica are distinguished by a top edging of scallops, usually enclosing a fertility goddess motif. Narrow hems were worn by older women and in some villages, while deeper ones were for festive or bridal wear and then usually incorporated gold threads.*

48 *Right: Cushion cover, Skyros, Greek Islands. Double darning in silk on fine linen. Typical figurative motifs of Sporades embroidery, usually attributed to Skyros, include ships, birds, figures and human-headed birds and animals.*

9 Front of woman's shirt, Sofia, Bulgaria. Cross stitch in cotton thread on cotton fabric. Red with black outlining and small hooks is typical of Bulgaria.

0 Right: Woman's sleeveless jerkin, Hungary. Satin and buttonhole in silk on sheepskin. Sheepskin and leather garments were made by artisans of the Carpathians.

1 Below: Purse, Mezőkövesd, Hungary. Satin stitch in wool on woollen fabric. The detached flowerhead with an encircling leaf is known as the 'Matyó' rose pattern.

2 Fragment, Mezőkövesd, Hungary. Satin stitch in cotton on linen. The Matyó rose motif often clearly shows its origin in the Turkish saz motif of a flowerhead surrounded by a curving bell-hung stem or leaf.

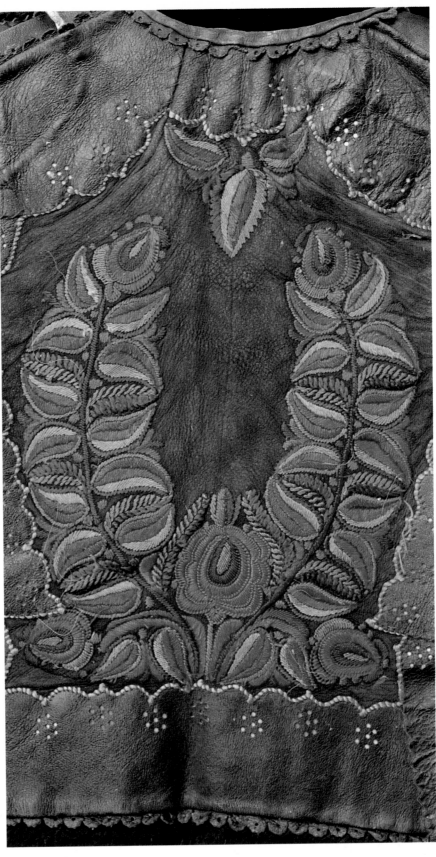

53 Married woman's bonnet, Piešťany, Slovakia. The combination of broderie anglaise, bobbin lace and floral brocaded ribbon – here lining the hem of the bonnet – are typical of Czechoslovakian embroidery.

54 Bedcurtain, kutnice, Trnava, Slovakia. Pulled threadwork with satin stitch. To protect the mother and newborn child from evil spirits both were confined for forty days behind an embroidered curtain. Pulledwork enabled the mother to see into the room and the designs were usually symbolic, here the tulip of fertility.

55 Man's sleeveless jacket, Trenčianské Teplá, Slovakia. Chain stitch in silk, red zigzag appliquéd edging on black wool. Patterns on the woollen garments of Eastern Europe were generally more archaic than those on linen.

56 Opposite: Marriage handkerchief, Russia. Gold thread on fine linen. Handkerchiefs were traditionally embroidered in most of northern and Eastern Europe by the bride, to give to special wedding guests.

CANDINAVIA

7   Bench cushion, Denmark. Chain, stem
nd satin stitch in wool on wool. The tree of
fe is in the form of a vase with the flowers
f fertility: the tulip, carnation and rose.

WESTERN EUROPE

8   Man's waistcoat, France, first half
ghteenth century. Tamboured chain stitch
n silk on silk. Such waistcoats were made all
ver Europe. To protect the English
mbroidery industry imports were forbidden
nd were burned. This one is stamped:
ustoms House Seized Dover GR II.

9   Cloth, Navalcan, Spain. Monochrome
lk on cotton. The villagers believed the
byrinth pattern to have magic powers.

0   Purse, Viana do Castelo, Minho,
ortugal. Beads, sequins, satin stitch in silk
vist on velvet. The word amor is typical of
ortuguese embroidery.

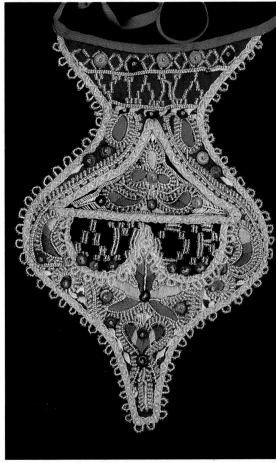

61 Crazy patchwork lap quilt, England, 1898. Silk and velvet sequins, beads, varied stitchery. Randomly patched quilts were popular in North America and in England.

NORTH AMERICA

62 Triple pouch, Ojibwa or Ottawa tribes, North America. Quillwork on smoked skin. The thunderbird is a mythological creature associated with rain and fertility.

CENTRAL AMERICA

63 Woman's blouse front, mola, Kuna Blas Indian, Panama. Layered and cut cotton appliqué. Mola designs are taken from local mythology and contemporary life.

Mainland Greece, Yugoslavia and Albania

In spite of the ethnic complexity of this region and its exuberantly colourful costume, underlying themes can be discerned. Geometric pattern in counted thread embroidery, often in wool and combined with drawn threadwork, decorates the edges, especially the cuffs, of Dinaric-cut linen shifts. In Greece, shifts are often sleeveless and may be of indigo cotton or of wool. The white linen ones of Attica have a deep band of dense stitchery at the hem, featuring stylized fertility goddesses.

In the mountains of western Yugoslavia embroidery is in cross or darning stitch, in copper, blue and green wool. Further north patterns are more floral and Pannonian blouses and skirts of white linen replace shifts. Headscarves or hanging headdresses are embroidered with flowers in multicoloured silks or in geometric cross stitch; knitted socks and gloves with geometric patterns and beadwork; and felted woollen jackets and coats with sun discs, spirals, the tree of life, and braidwork. In Thrace woollen aprons and dresses are in the same archaic style. Dazzling appendages to ward off evil spirits supplement embroidery on most costume, especially in Yugoslavia. Urban embroidery is in Turkish style: goldwork coats and floral towels for the house.

Bulgaria

The linen undershift of Bulgarian costume, worn with overdress, woven apron, headscarf and Turkish goldwork jacket, is distinguished by the discreetly patterned embroidery on its hem, front bodice and sleeves, each being in a different design and material: a dense geometric counted thread on the sleeve in cotton, for example, may accompany more open stylized plant patterns in wool at the hem. The cut is either Dinaric with a small mandarin collar, or has a side-buttoning neck opening and smocked bodice centre front and back, with straight sleeves embroidered in one band at the hem and another halfway up. With this cut the embroidery appears on the bodice front, shoulder and in a vertical panel on the sleeve. Colours are sombre, with soft red predominating; stitches are cross, diagonal, and double running for the small hook patterns common around motifs, and crochet and *oya* edgings are frequent. Woollen coats with archaic patterning are also to be found, and tasselled hanging head-dresses.

Rumania

Characteristic of Rumanian embroidery is a fine sense of balance: a full richly embroidered blouse is worn with a straight dark woven skirt and apron, areas of dense stitchery alternate with fine open linear patterning, dark colours with light, cross stitch in silk with chain stitch in metal.

Most important is the blouse of Pannonian cut in crinkly white fabric, originally linen but from the nineteenth century cotton. The disposition of the embroidery is particular: the most solid work is over the shoulder, the bottom part of the sleeve is lightly embroidered in diagonal or vertical lines of isolated motifs and the two areas are separated by a narrow contrasting band usually of drawn threadwork or pale quilting. Patterns are geometric or occasionally floral. In Transylvania costume is of heavy linen worked in black and white stitchery and drawn threadwork.

Sometimes petticoats or shifts are embroidered, also headscarves, men's shirts in whitework, and cushions to be displayed with the clothing in the best room of the house on occasions such as marriage. Sheepskin and woollen coats are professionally embroidered in floral patterns throughout the entire Carpathian region.

Hungary

The embroidered sheepskin cloak of the shepherds of Eastern Europe 'serves as chair and bed for a man of peasant type. One can eat on its surface and dry meat upon it; and if a growing lad is bundled into it, three days' fever will pass away. Best of all a beautifully embroidered suba *decorated with chamois is a festive cloak to parade in on Sundays.'*

Hungarian embroidery is epitomized by repeat chunky flowerheads in heavy cotton or wool thread – tulips, pomegranates, roses, carnations, rosettes – of Turkish inspiration, but small birds may enliven the work. Satin is the most common stitch, often combined with white drawn threadwork, and monochrome square chain stitch, originating from the region of Kalotaszeg now in Rumania, is also popular. On costume bright colours are worn by the young, and sombre by older people. Best known is the floral work of Mezőkövesd which was commercialized at the turn of the century and attracted attention abroad in the wake of the English Crafts Movement.

The glory of Hungarian embroidery is the floral work on sheepskin jackets, coats and cloaks, and on woollen frieze coats. Traditionally worked in white and red leather appliqué in patterns of oriental origin, embroidery in silk and wool gradually overran the old designs.

On linen clothing the sleeves of shifts and blouses are the most important area of embroidery. They are extremely full and gathered into the shoulder, upon which the embroidery stretches across the upper arm in a band, usually in heavy geometric patterning combined with whitework – a style in which the hems of aprons, skirts and petticoats are also embroidered. Kerchiefs are normally of fine whitework or of white appliqué like a paper cutout. Bedlinen was embroidered with motifs of flowers and birds.

Czechoslovakia

The country of Czechoslovakia is a political coupling of East and West. In Bohemia in the west embroidery on costume was long ago replaced by purchased ribbons, trimmings and an excessive use of machine broderie anglaise. Only scarves and aprons of whitework, with white bobbin lace trim, are significant. In south-eastern Moravia and Slovakia in the east, embroidery is mainly on blouses and aprons and can be identified by the presence of coloured bobbin lace, brocaded floral ribbon and broderie anglaise. The blouses are of Pannonian cut, with or without a shoulder seam, and often reach only just below the bust. The sleeves are very full with a flounced cuff and are often intricately pleated; collars are also embroidered and are usually of mandarin style with a ruff of ribbon, bobbin lace or needleweaving. In Kyjov, Moravia, they are sailor style, embroidered with black floral patterns.

Pleated skirts, open at the centre front, are usually embroidered in geometric pattern along the back waistband, and are worn with an apron worked with natural flower patterns. Bonnets are worked in the same particular village style as the blouse. Men's linen shirts have heavily stitched bands of geometric patterning and floral motifs on sleeves and neck placket.

Typical techniques are broderie anglaise in yellow and orange of the Piešťany region; satin stitch patterns in bright colours combined with drawn threadwork of Čičmany; metal thread stitchery with whitework of Trnava; tamboured cutwork of Detva and Zvolen; bright woolwork of Rybany; and Slav knot stitch in yellow and orange of Moravia. Patterns are geometric and floral, but can also portray confronting birds and the tree of life.

Sheepskin coats are appliquéd in coloured or red leather or have floral embroidery, less flamboyant than Hungary. Felted wool coats are decorated with archaic motifs, including horn-derived hearts, and braiding and pompoms. Men's woollen trousers are embroidered on the front pockets with flowers, a style that extends from Poland as far west as south Germany.

Eastern Slovakia, the Ukraine and Poland

Linen shirts made by girls for their own trousseau and for their bridegrooms are the most important embroidered article of this mainly trans-Carpathian region. Motifs are normally flowers of cross stitch in bright colours. In the Carpathians themselves sheepskin and woollen coats, and in Poland also men's woollen trousers, are embroidered with floral designs. In the Ukraine long linen towels with goddess figures or flowers at each end are used ceremonially in the home.

The Russian heartland

In Russia such towels were hung at crossroads, from birch trees and in the home around icons and mirrors. Here motifs are almost always figurative, usually in red, depicting the earth goddess and mythological figures, but later towels are tamboured in polychrome with contemporary people. Aprons, too, sometimes have the same motifs. Linen bedcurtains and wedding sheets are worked with a deep border drawn into a squared grid and darned with scenes in white or colour, often edged with bobbin lace.

Costume carries less embroidery than elsewhere in northern and Eastern Europe. Linen shifts are Pannonian in cut, or Dinaric with side neck opening, or have a skirt gathered into a high waist. Embroidery is almost entirely in red in bands across the sleeve, cuff, neck placket and hem and is alternated with strips of brocaded weaving or appliquéd fabrics also in red.

Goldwork features on the stiff padded roll worn round the midriff and on the headdresses, which differ in shape with each region. Pearls abound, as they do on Russian ecclesiastical embroidery. Other Russian embroidery is in the Western European tradition.

SCANDINAVIA

'M K Anno 1680'; 'BJE 1756': such inscriptions on Swedish cushions betray the Western influence on Scandinavian embroidery and thus a motivation that is entirely different from embroidery conforming to social customs and beliefs. It is personal and in the fashion of its time. Pattern books from Italy and Germany were disseminated from the seventeenth century throughout Scandinavia. Festive linen – bedcovers, and hangings, pillow cases, towels, shirts, aprons, scarves – is embroidered with mainly pattern-book motifs in drawn threadwork and red cross stitch.

Localized traditional embroidery is mainly in wool. Bed- and wall-hangings, cushions for the hard wooden benches of peasant homes, and also for sleighs, are roughly worked in shaded wools in long satin stitch, in Sweden sometimes with added French knots. Motifs depict flower sprays, tulips, roses, carnations, pomegranates and 8-pointed stars with small birds, horses, deer and figures, usually arranged around a central motif and closely resembling the decoration on carved and painted peasant furniture. In Norway such floral embroidery can be seen on headdresses, skirts and bodices, where the flowers are mainly depicted without stems, very much in Hungarian style. In Iceland they are worked in split stitch and decorate the hem of festive woollen dresses.

Pattern darning is an old technique found in Iceland and on the coffin covers of Telemark in Norway. Appliqué is another, and is used on pockets to hang from a belt, and on cushions in Sweden; along with tin thread embroidery, it is also the technique used by the Lapps. They edge their bright blue wool costume in red with touches of white, yellow and green. In Karelia, the eastern part of Finland, linen shifts are embroidered in oriental style with hooked and serrated pattern.

WESTERN EUROPE

Though the coif of peasant costume lingered in Western Europe women used commercial textiles in preference to embroidery. Cashmere shawls were among those sold by itinerant peddlars in nineteenth-century rural France.

Dating and naming, rather than geographical location, is the key factor in identifying the embroidery of the West. It is an ecclesiastical and urban tradition, a professional or leisure occupation subject to fashion and trade and is not rooted in beliefs and social customs; as such it is outside the scope of this book.

The general availability of commercial materials and the pattern books published from 1523 onwards and sold throughout Europe impart a certain unity to embroidery from Scandinavia to Spain. Urban and court fashions were copied assiduously by the prosperous middle class almost everywhere. But for the peasants of Western Europe, subjected to sumptuary laws forbidding the decoration of costume, it was the French Revolution which brought prosperity and freedom. They, too, began to copy urban fashions but mainly with materials available commercially – few had to produce their own, as in Eastern Europe. Outer clothing was thus usually decorated with ribbons and trimmings and handwork was lavished on whitework coifs, aprons and fichus, on goldwork bonnets, and on red cross stitch embroidery on linen.

Only in isolated regions – mountain valleys, for example – did embroidery survive with its old purpose (and in some areas, Brittany in particular, it was used to show affiliation to a group). The urban and ecclesiastical embroidery of Spain and Portugal was in the mainstream of the West, but relative geographical isolation from Europe ensured that most embroidery of the Iberian peninsula was traditional.

Spain With Sicily, Spain was the Arab and Islamic gateway to Europe, and this is reflected in the hallmark of Spanish embroidery: intricate patterning executed in simple stitchery and limited colouring. The background fabric is usually linen and the threads black wool, honey and blue linen, or red or green floss silk, used to make men's shirts and pants, women's blouses and shifts, offertory and funeral cloths and display linen for the marriage bed. All come from the region to the west and south of Madrid, although there are marked differences in the work of each town or village: examples are the monochrome latticed patterning in the darning stitch of Navalcan and the Assisi work in floss silk, especially on the shoulders, neck and cuffs of shirts or blouses of the Sierra Morena. The cut is usually straight with a curved or square neckline and full sleeves, often smocked into neck and cuff. Linen shirts for the bridegroom are beautifully worked over the front bodice with white drawn threadwork and needleweaving, often in honey silk or linen threads, and with red cross stitch initials below the neck opening. The finest come from Lagartera in Toledo province, where the blouses have black wool spirals down each side of the front, surrounded by small repeat motifs of floral derivation. Salamancan women's blouses have full sleeves displaying Asian motifs of animals with reserve pattern worked in black, and on cloths the same motifs appear in pastel colours.

The linen Renaissance bands of Avila, inserted into household and ecclesiastical hangings, can be distinguished from those of Azemmour in Morocco by their stitch and colour. The patterns are the same tree of life or vase flanked by birds left in reserve, but the background is either black wool in darning, or soft green, blue or red silk in cross stitch, pulled thread or reversible tent stitch, where Azemmour bands are in long-armed cross. Motifs are outlined in self colour or black.

'Spanish' shawls were originally imported from Manila and then copied in workshops in Andalucia. They are simpler and brighter than the Chinese.

Portugal Portugal is the only country of Western Europe where embroidery is still a significant commercial activity. The leitmotif is sentimentality: linen production was suffused with symbolism of love and fidelity, and the main motifs on linen garments are hearts and flowers, coats of arms, the word *amor*, initials and dates, always worked in red. The stitches used are satin, cross and pulledwork, with bullion and eyelet in Guimarães, in colours of red, white and blue. The most common articles so decorated are bridegrooms' shirts, worked over the front bodice in white stitchery, with a red motto below; womens' blouses, which have much simpler work, usually blue embroidery and smocking at the shoulder; and linen for display on the marriage bed and washbasin. The sweetheart hankies of Minho have mottoes and vows of love worked in red.

From Portugal's role as a trading nation come the embroidered carpets of Arraiolos still made today, which are copies of imported Persian ones. A border in two colours, usually sludge and blue, but occasionally chestnut red, is contrasted with a field in reverse colour order. The Persian designs were later replaced by animals and flowers.

Bedcovers of Castelo Branco are of strips of linen embroidered with patterns derived from Indian palampores in laid couched floss silks. Focus of the design is a central medallion, often enclosing a couple, or a tree, surrounded by a riot of flowers and birds. Their source was the Indo-Portuguese quilts of the seventeenth century – works of art depicting scenes from Indian mythology or the Bible.

NORTH AMERICA

Quilts, born of the necessity to utilize every scrap of precious fabric, and of the pleasure of social gathering in a frontier society, are the cream of American needlework. Embroidery, in general, followed the fashions of Western Europe, with a slight time-lag, interpreting them in a more limited vocabulary of stitches, simpler designs and cruder materials, with a consequent gain in vitality and charm. Sampler and needlepoint are particularly revered.

Not only did Americans follow the fashion of Europe, but the Indian tribes as well, who adopted the floral motifs of European embroidery. The geometric and mythological patterns of moosehair and porcupine quillwork were gradually replaced by pretty pastel flowers in commercial beads, on cloth as well as on the indigenous skin and bark. An enormous range of articles was embroidered, including coats, shirts, moccasins, gloves, saddles, pouches and bags. By the early eighteenth century there was already a market for trinkets, such as boxes, scissor-cases and sundry 'native fancy goods'.

CENTRAL AMERICA

From Maya, Aztec, Inca and even earlier civilizations comes one of the finest traditions of weaving in the world, still continued by many women of Central and South America. Decoration on their untailored clothing of handwoven cotton or wool – tunics, shawls, wrap-around skirts, and sashes – is usually brocaded and embroidery is only introduced as weaving skill declines.

Mexico

Embroidery is normally on factory-made cloth and is European-inspired. Thus the traditional tunics (*huipils*) and shawls (*quechquémitls*) of Mexico

Girls of Chichicastenango sit in the market selling brightly embroidered blouses ready to be sewn up. Their wrapped woven clothing has alternating colour along the seams, a device found in many parts of the world.

are brocaded with geometric patterns and with stylized sacred animals and birds, but the white cotton blouses, with square necks and short sleeves of European cut, are embroidered with massed large motifs of flowers, birds, animals combined with 8-pointed stars, all mixed together in a riot of gaudy colours in satin stitch (although crochet edges are commonly in white). Flouncy dresses with brilliant flowers and gold-embroidered suits are reminiscent of the bullfights and fiestas of Andalucia.

On some garments more sober negative patterning and cross stitch designs following the weft recall brocading techniques. Styles vary and, though men's clothing is usually plain, some festive shirts and bags – necessary as clothing has no pockets – are embroidered with geometric motifs and animals.

Guatemala

The great strength of Guatemalan textiles is supplementary weft weaving: stylized birds and animals of sharp diagonal lines, combined with plant forms and zigzags symbolizing the serpent, in sophisticated colourings, embellish clothing of stitched straight loom widths. Embroidery, symbolic or floral on *huipils*, is far less significant.

Panama

Unique in the world are the blouse fronts, known as *molas*, of the Kuna Indians of Panama, worked by a complicated technique of layering. Of brightly coloured cotton with red predominating, slit to disclose patching of varied hues, they depict local mythology, birds and animals, and often images derived from the modern world such as cigar boxes and political slogans.

SOUTH AMERICA

The textiles of Bolivia and Peru perpetrate the superb weaving skills of the Incas and earlier peoples – symbols of the sun, the sacred condor, serpent and jaguar are woven and not embroidered. Yet in the Paracas region on

Embroideries from the necropolis of Paracas in Peru bear the same motifs as the mysterious Nazca Lines cut into the desert. The figure with bristly head on a shirt, unku, is similar to three figures cut into a hillside in the Ingenio valley, and the feline motif on a mantle is echoed in the enormous figure drawn on the desert near the town of Ica.

the Peruvian coast were discovered in 1925 some of the oldest embroideries in the world. This arid desert peninsula was a necropolis for the local community from about 600 to 200 BC. They buried their dead élite, prepared for the next world, in mummy bundles containing often hundreds of textiles, mainly woven but also embroidered in vivid wools in loop and stem stitch. The motifs depict felines, serpents, birds of prey, killer whales and human forms intermingled in a contorted maze of appendages, with weapons and trophy heads – images conveying mythological beliefs and ritual and social obligations that remain mystifying. They resemble some of the huge animals cut in outline in the nearby desert, which are interspersed among giant straight lines visible only from the air: the puzzling Nazca Lines of unknown sacred or astronomical purpose. Such is the richness of the Paracas textiles that the lives and wealth of the living must have been almost entirely dedicated to serving the dead.

◆◆◆◆◆◆◆◆◆◆◆◆◆◆◆◆◆◆

2
THE DECORATIVE
POWER OF CULT

THE GREAT GODDESS
Identification of a cult source

Certain guidelines can be observed in determining when the purpose and pattern of tribal and peasant embroidery are mythological in origin. The patterns are likely to appear on articles associated with some ritual or rite of passage, such as marriage or death, or with something of symbolic significance, such as a woman's hair. The embroideries often come from an isolated or ethnically different area of a country, like the northern wastes of Russia or the 'barbarian' provinces of China. An embroidered female figure is usually goddess-derived, rather than merely a depiction of a woman, if she is accompanied by other mythological symbols, such as zigzags, birds, chevrons or toads, or by a worshipping figure. She will normally form part of a repeat symmetrical pattern or be one herself, portrayed in a ritual stance, often with the suggestion of a held branch. The deformation of figures – women that are half trees, or birds, or bees, or that have a base like an idol rather than legs – also usually indicates a cult origin.

Such symbolism, however, is not clear-cut. Primitive mythology is a complex attempt to grasp the concepts of fertility, life, death and cosmic creation and cannot be categorized into a series of separate cults. So patterns from different sources merge: the fertility goddess can be transfigured into a tree of life or bestowed with horns, the moon is a goddess or is male, the sun is a hunter or a life-giver. Myths overlap or oppose in different cultures, some disseminated through movement of peoples, most generated from the same basic human needs and instincts, surviving for millennia. The mythology of the great goddess persisted to classical Greece and was then absorbed into Greek legend, passing eventually into Christianity as the cult of the Virgin Mary.

The goddess figure on an Archaic-Cypriot jug of 700–600 BC and on East Greek metal plaques of 720–520 BC is accompanied by mythological symbols also found on later embroidered examples.

Origins of the goddess cult

The concept of the earth as a bearing and nourishing mother is almost universal: in every early society, practically without exception, a myth exists recounting the creation of the universe. Usually it embodies the idea

65

The lozenge shape of the Lespugue ivory Venus of the Aurignacian period (30,000–25,000 BC) is echoed in the embroideries of Bekalta in Tunisia and the wedge-shaped head of the Mycenaean goddess of 1300–1200 BC in the embroidery of Russian ritual towels.

The goddess in embroidery

The bird goddess or siren forms an East Greek terracotta perfume bottle of 640 BC and is in the shape of the fabled sirens of Russian pagan mythology, Sirine and Alconoste.

of a static life-producing earth in the form of a goddess, fertilized by an active, stimulating, penetrating manifestation of the male thrust, such as a bird (a link between heaven and earth), or a serpent or toad.

Mankind's earliest sculptures – cult figurines dating from the palaeolithic period of about 30,000 BC and made of mammoth ivory – are of this goddess: earth mother, source of life, symbol of fertility. From the neolithic period of about 5000 BC onwards such figurines are found in quantity in Asia and the Near East, in the pre-Indo-European matriarchal society of Old Europe and in the Cycladic, Minoan and Mycenaean civilizations. The figurines, of terracotta or bronze, come mainly from graves and sanctuaries and their precise purpose is not known. Those at sanctuaries seem mostly to have been votive offerings, left perhaps as substitutes for sacrifices or in place of worshippers. Some were left at domestic shrines where they were placed to guard both hearth and home. All may not be representations of the goddess but rather of a priestess or human worshipper. Often they are decorated with red, symbolizing the mystery of blood.

These figurines were particularly common in Old Europe, which extended from the Adriatic and Aegean to the Ukraine and Poland, and it is especially in the Mediterranean region and in Russia that goddess figures predominate in embroidery. Pagan mythology survived in the Mediterranean to the period of classical Greece when much was absorbed from the earlier Aegean civilizations, and Greece accepted most of the panoply of gods of the Thracians, citizens of the Achaemenid empire that stretched eastward to the Hindu Kush. They worshipped the earth goddess and featured her, riding a lioness, on their silverwork of the fourth century BC. Not surprisingly, Greek embroidery has many examples of figures derived from the earth goddess, such as those holding branches, common on the cushion covers and towels of Skyros in the Cyclades, home of a flourishing civilization in the third millennium BC. Seated figures holding branches are also worked on cushions and bed valances from Epirus in north-western Greece, a region that was Roman, Byzantine and then a prosperous Turkish province. In Attica the hems of the women's shifts are decorated almost entirely with simplified versions of the goddess.

In early figurines the goddess was depicted with extended egg-shaped buttocks giving her a bird-like appearance, which was accentuated by a beak. The association of the goddess with birds was strong and features frequently in embroideries. In Skyros she is half bird in form and in Russia the bird sirens known as Sirine and Alconoste have female faces and exotic plumage. They are the birds of ancient fable who charmed the saints in paradise with their singing.

The oldest surviving textile depicting a manifestation of the goddess is the great felt found in one of the tombs of Pazyryk in the Altai mountains of southern Siberia. Over the centuries rain seeped into these burial

The seated goddess holding a sacred branch and approached by a rider, depicted on the great felt of Pazyryk, is a motif found in various guises and derivations in the embroideries of many countries.

chambers, even poured in where robbers had left open shafts, and then froze solid, preserving in deep freeze objects dating from the seventh to the second century BC, the felt among them. Repeated across its width is the motif of a seated goddess figure holding a sacred branch. She is believed to be Tabiti, deity of the hearth and therefore of fire and fertility, worshipped in Russia in pre-Scythian times. She is approached by a male rider on a horse, possibly a worshipper. In later embroidered depictions of the goddess in many countries she is frequently associated with a mounted horseman.

The anthropomorphic figures of Western embroidery are not goddess-derived but normally come from the Bible or from engravings or prints, or are of contemporary scenes. However, in the 1930s a new motif appeared in English embroidery: the crinoline lady. The thatched cottages and hollyhocks that accompanied her sprang from nostalgia for an imagined simple rural life, aroused by the ribbon development and suburban sprawl then taking place. But the lady herself was an anachronism. It was not nineteenth-century fashion plates that were being copied by embroider-esses then but peasant work that conveyed the same idyll of security in a changing world. Might the origins of the lady not also perhaps be traced, through more obvious examples in peasant embroidery, to the same fertility myths going back to palaeolithic times?

Stance: raised arms

The stance of the goddess was everywhere of ritual significance. Often she is portrayed with arms raised or legs outspread or in a frontal pose with symmetrical excrescences of animal or plant form at her sides.

Raising the arms is an instinctive gesture of self-defence and an imprinted one of surrender. It is also associated with worship and for primitive peoples, such as the pigmies, with supplication to the sun. Mayan gods raised their arms to hold up the sky. It is always an important gesture of dance – bird-headed dancing women, so postured, are in the Aurignacian rock-paintings of Pêche Merle in France. Dancing often implied imitation of animal movements and therefore identity with them.

A terracotta figurine of the goddess with raised arms, from Razgrad, Bulgaria, dates from around 4000 BC. Later Minoan and Mycenaean figurines also feature the goddess in this stance. It became a very common embroidery motif.

In embroidery the motif of a female figure with upraised arms is common almost everywhere. She resembles early terracotta goddess figurines, for example those of neolithic Iberia, Egypt, Old Europe and India. The same form appears in Tunisia as an ancient carving, a modern embroidery motif and a ritual of the marriage ceremony. There the Phoenician carvings on the stelae of Carthage, showing the goddess Tanit with raised or outstretched arms, often simplified and stylized to a circle with linear hands on a triangular base, are matched in embroidery on women's marriage garments. These depict the earth goddess and are also a rendering in embroidery of the modern bride at her *jelwa* – at this presentation ceremony on the fourth day of the wedding the bride is veiled and dressed as an idol in seven tunics, the outer one heavily embroidered and stiff with gold, topped with goldwork boleros, a coif and all the jewelry of her dowry. For this climax of the seven-day marriage ceremony she stands on a platform, her arms raised and the palm of her hand turned to the assembled guests to be unveiled in their presence. After this the marriage is consummated. This ritual is understood to originate in a long-lost fertility rite and is supposed to avert the evil eye – the hands here are raised for protection. It clearly dates back to the Phoenician worship of the goddess, though the embroidery motif is normally described as 'the bride at her *jelwa*' rather than as the goddess Tanit.

The heartland of Russia and the Ukraine retained until early this century ritual embroideries whose pagan origins are clear both in their uses and motifs. The Russian ceremonial towels, hung at crossroads and on birch trees, are decorated with archaic motifs, the most common of which is the goddess, arms raised in supplication and often with huge hands to avert evil. The same motifs are on Ukrainian towels called *rushnyky*, hung around icons and crosses or on the walls of houses to fend off evil.

Western European embroideries have many examples of female figures with raised arms. These are normally interpreted as representing dancing women or the wise and foolish virgins, possibly a Christianized version of the pagan motif.

Stance: outspread legs

The goddess with outspread legs, flanked by lions, features on a bronze Etruscan chariot and lingers in both female and male form in Italian art of the sixteenth century.

The stance with outspread legs, the body opened like a book exposing the genitals in a birth-giving posture, is found in almost all primitive art and was sifted through Renaissance pattern into the decorative arts of Europe as a two-tailed mermaid creature, sometimes with a masculine face. As such it is common, for example, on the embroidered skirts of Crete.

The same posture of splayed legs denotes the toad, a symbol of fertility. Conception was not understood by primitive man and as a miscarried foetus resembles a toad, these creatures were believed to crawl into the womb to fertilize the woman. They were considered a protection against barrenness and are still votive offerings to Mary in south-eastern Europe.

The addition of an appendage between the legs confuses the imagery still further. It is then usually intended to convey a lizard, worshipped like the snake for its skin-shedding, a symbol of the renewal of life. Shapes with splayed legs and raised arms that are a confused medley of male and female anthropomorphism, toad and lizard are embroidered on coats of the Iban people of Borneo. These probably belonged to medicine men, whose powers would be evident in the motifs on their clothing. Such motifs, surrounded by other lizard-like creatures, are worked in cowrie shells on the skirts of Sumba in Indonesia. These skirts were an important part of the woman's dowry and were also often used as grave gifts and buried with her.

In her role as life-giver the goddess is most frequently shown frontally with animals, plants and insects growing out of or surrounding her body. Her wide skirt, possibly denoting the huge buttocks and stomach of early

Minoan seals of 1700–1450 BC are engraved with a lizard-like creature and the fish and axe associated with creation.

figurines, is often surrounded by or filled with birds, animals or 'daughter' goddesses. Bronze figurines of Luristan dating from about 1000 BC depict creatures as an integral part of her body whereas in the depictions on archaic Greek vases they are generally arranged in an orderly fashion around her. In early Iranian art she was also shown as queen of the beasts, holding animals at her sides. As fertility goddess she projects her powers through plants and animals – their presence with her on embroideries helps identify her, as do added cosmic symbols such as the swastika or the double axe.

Acolytes

Ritual mounted worshippers feature on peasant Chinese embroidery and as Greek terracotta figurines of 580–550 BC.

The mother goddess in the Indian form, Devi, is depicted riding on an elephant and on a Turkish towel she is transmuted into a column, flanked by a mounted worshipper.

The animals that symbolized the goddess's fertility became in later art her acolytes: she was shown flanked by birds, dogs or lions, or approached by riders offering sacred branches or baskets of fruit, as in Sumerian art of the fourth to third millennium BC. A derivation of this theme is the so-called boxer motif on seventeenth-century English samplers.

The mounted horseman in scenes of the hunt is portrayed in a naturalistic way, but when he is of mythological origin he is stylized, often with arms raised in the votive position. Bent legs are frequently one of the characteristics of the horse; the animal alone with such bent legs appears on Russian towels and Dutch samplers. This distortion cannot be attributed merely to their counted thread technique.

The horse itself – a favourite animal, for example, in Nordic pre-Christian mythology – is replaced in many instances by a more exotic creature, such as a bull, dragon, elephant, cock or cat. The Indian mother goddess, Devi, herself rides on an elephant on the embroideries of Kutch and Gujarat and the *kanthas* of Bengal.

In Minoan and Old European mythology a column was an incarnation of the goddess, rather than a cosmogonic symbol forming the axis of the world as in other cultures. As such she was flanked by rampant lions or griffins, to form a motif disseminated through Europe by the Renaissance pattern books. More commonly she is transfigured as a tree rather than a column, with guardian or worshipping animals or birds, forming an axis between the waters of earth and the heavens.

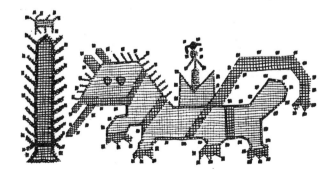

Associated symbols

The associations of the goddess are manifold. Water is a major one, with the mystery of life represented by the waters of birth – and thus of cosmic creation – expressed in chevron and meander patterning. The ship is the sheltering vessel through the sea of life and a common embroidery motif. Mermaids are guardians of the waters, often with mirror in hand, and are a motif of seventeenth-century English samplers. Fish symbolize the waters' power as the origin and preserver of life and are often the emblem of the soul. In Bengal fish are embroidered on *kanthas* as a fertility symbol for a marriageable daughter. A felt hanging dating from about the first century BC, found at Noin Ula in Mongolia, is embroidered with turtles and fish, hardly familiar creatures in the Gobi desert. Crocodiles are also frequently venerated for their association with spirits, who are presumed, like the crocodile, to reside in hidden dark corners of rivers.

Rainwaters bringing life and fertility to animals and crops were associated with the milk of the goddess and symbolized by parallel lines and triangles. The appearance of these patterns on the breasts of goddess figurines made during a prolonged dessication of the earth's atmosphere in the sixth millennium BC suggests such an association. Modern wedding dresses of Sada'a in northern Yemen have such triangles and lines embroidered on the breasts.

Fertility

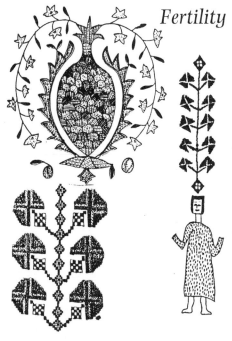

Symbols of fertility include the pomegranate – a ubiquitous motif which was probably also the apple of the Garden of Eden – and the carnation. The Syrian stylized row of carnations known as 'railway lines' is already found in Coptic embroidery.

Marrows and apples piled for harvest thanksgiving at the altar of an English church, decorated eggs at Easter, the biblical scourge of the barren woman – fecundity of soil and woman has always been a primary concern of mankind. The earliest sacred precinct was where women gave birth and is symbolized by a lozenge, often with a central dot. Figurines of the goddess in Old Europe have this pattern, often divided into four, incised on the stomach or the head. It is a device found also in embroidery.

Symbols that express fruitfulness are almost universal and so common-place as to have lost their original meaning. Most obvious is the pomegranate with its viscous blood-red seeds. In embroidery it is often transmuted from the rose encircled by a bell-hung or serrated leaf of the *saz* style of Turkish art. Although in the West the tulip is probably embroidered merely as a precious flower, with its shape akin to the female vulva it is another symbol of fertility in other cultures, and is often associated with the pomegranate, as is the carnation. The carnation is the most frequent motif in the embroidery of northern Syria, symbolized into a hexagon and barely recognizable as a flower. This Syrian pattern is matched in a Christian Coptic embroidery of the early Middle Ages. All the motifs on it are religious: crosses, inscriptions, a figure – possibly St George – killing a dragon, and naïve people apparently in positions of adoration. The carnation motif may therefore also have had some religious significance.

Fundamental symbol of female fecundity is of course the pubic triangle, exaggerated in primitive figurines and depicted alone in prehistoric rock-painting. So commonplace as a geometric pattern it has retained virtually no vestige of symbolic meaning, except when used as a potent talisman. Embroidered triangles, like silver amulets, are frequently hung on children's caps, over the ear. The protective power of the triangle is also invoked in the appliquéd chevrons of striped fabric used to edge embroidered costume in many countries.

THE TREE OF LIFE

The tree of life is one of the most common motifs in embroidery almost everywhere. Whereas the great goddess is the unrecognized source of many an anthropomorphic motif, almost every vaguely foliate shape and every pot of flowers is deemed to represent the tree of life. Most in fact do.

The tree is one of the most potent of symbols. Its roots delve into the underworld, its trunk links the earth to the heavens – it transcends all three spheres. Its life-cycle unfurls before our eyes in each season of the year, the symbolism of birth, maturity, death and rebirth embodied in leaf, bud and fruit. Its fruitfulness is matched by the fruitfulness of woman and even sap and milk were equated by primitive man.

Versions of the tree of life are manifold but it is this fertility and consequent embodying of the goddess with attendant worshippers or guardians that is the one most commonly found in embroidery. The tree can, however, also be depicted as a half-goddess, a vase of flowers, a fountain or a symbol from local iconography, such as an eagle or a heart. It may be a simple linear pattern intended to signify a particular tree, such as a palm, or more often to convey the general concept of growth and fertility. When the tree of life is depicted as an actual tree it is stylized to convey its mythological significance. Consequently foliate patterns or simple branched devices signify the tree of life, rather than a realistic tree with trunk and leafy branches.

The palm-leaf pattern of a Cretan gold pendant of 1700–1500 BC remains a common form of the tree of life motif.

Tcheremiss people of Siberia in festive dress return from a sacrificial grove. Hanging embroideries from trees and sacrificing beads to the gods were common customs in parts of Russia.

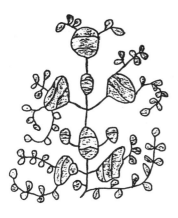

This version of the tree of life on a dress from Qutayfé in Syria is also found on the peasant embroideries of Korea.

The goddess tree

A tree is left growing from a Calcutta pavement and converted into an altar to be venerated by passers-by.

The goddess with raised arms, transmuted into a tree or plant form, is evident on the cuffs of a burial shift from Martovce in Czechoslovakia.

The tree of life in the guise of a plant form with every leaf split into different colours is found in the *min-soo* peasant work of Korea, in the embroidery of southern Syria, where sacred trees were worshipped by the Phoenicians, and in Hungary and Portugal. These plant forms are often in the form of a cross, and trees were linked to the magic power of crossroads. The cross is but one aspect of the tree at the centre of the universe, the *axis mundi*, a mythology dating from the fourth or third millennium BC and especially important to Nordic and Central Asiatic races. From the tree as a central pillar the cross radiated to the four corners of the universe. In Yugoslavia the pre-Slav veneration of tree and pillar was still observed in the early years of this century. The tree as a pillar is rare in embroidery, though some Renaissance versions of this motif are worked in the monochrome bands of Sicily, Azemmour in Morocco, Parga in Greece and Avila in Spain, used for display around the home, or in the case of Avila incorporated into altar hangings.

The most primitive sacred place devised by man was an enclosure with tree, stone and water. The stone held the force of the goddess and the water symbolized her role in cosmic creation. Such enclosures were found in the Indus valley civilization of Mohenjo-daro of the second millennium BC and were still common in Buddha's time. Trees, with stones placed around them, are still venerated in India and will be enclosed even if they grow in the path of a road, which must then be detoured around them.

The tree symbolizing the goddess was a motif that appeared in the arts of the ancient civilizations of India, Mesopotamia, Egypt and the Aegean. It was often depicted flanked by worshippers or birds or by fabulous beasts in heraldic posture. From thence it found its way into decorative arts everywhere and can be claimed to be, in its several variations, the most common design of all. The animals can vary locally – the horse, for example, was popular as an object of pre-Christian cult – but in general they are fabled creatures such as dragons and griffins rather than familiar animals. In Islamic countries the fish is often added, and already appeared with the sacred tree in Mesopotamian art. Birds occur frequently, usually the symbolic peacock of oriental origin, or the cock, believed to drive away the spirits of the night and a symbol connected with solar mythology. The cosmic tree and goddess are also closely allied with the serpent, guardian of sanctuaries and the underworld and one of the most complex of symbols, associated also with rain and hair.

Ritual that linked the cult of the tree with the goddess survived in Russia and the Ukraine until the Second World War. A birch tree standing alone in a clearing was chosen to personify the goddess. It was then clothed in a woman's dress and the ritual towel was hung on one of its branches. Alternatively the towel would be suspended from a cross at the village crossroads. On these towels the goddess was depicted as such, or transmuted into a tree, but always embroidered in red. This transmutation is common in peasant embroidery, for example on the shift hems of the mountainous area of Stanke Dimitrov in Bulgaria. Similarly ambiguous are the cuffs of women's burial shifts of the village of Martovce in Czechoslovakia, cut in black taffeta around outspread hands and thus known as the 'four-fingered' motif.

Symbols replacing the tree

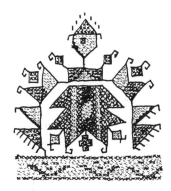

The goddess-tree becomes a plant on the shift hems of Stanke Dimitrov and Samokov in Bulgaria, but can still be recognized.

The goddess-tree was also symbolized by flowers and plants and water, as a never-ending process of creation. In Sumerian art the tree itself was replaced by the device of a plant growing from a vase. This version of the tree of life motif, still flanked by worshippers or guardians, is the favourite motif of the folk art of Europe. Significantly the flowers are always those associated with the earth goddess: the carnation, tulip and rose, often with added pomegranates. Sometimes, conveying the symbolism of water, a fountain replaces the vase and flowers.

Not only is the tree substituted by symbols pertaining to water (and therefore still to life and fertility), but in the embroideries of some countries it is also replaced by motifs from local iconography. The eagle, with one or two heads, is an example. This ancient solar symbol, representing the power of the sky gods, later a European heraldic emblem and device of the Habsburgs, can replace the tree in the embroideries of Spain and Russia, for instance, as can the heart in those of Central and Eastern Europe.

The inverted tree

The cosmic tree of primitive mythology was sometimes conceived as an inverted image, drawing strength through its roots in heaven and bestowing them on the world. At first glance the upside-down flower vases on a wedding dress of Thano Bula Khan in Sind would seem simply to indicate that the pattern had not been understood, but there are so many examples in embroidery of inverted renderings of the tree of life that it is most unlikely that all are merely mistaken. There are many upside-down versions of the pine or palm with a central trunk or spine and radiating lines. The date palm, venerated as a source of wealth, appears in this guise in many embroideries of the Arab world.

The tree of knowledge

The birth, life, death and regrowth of the tree symbolized in its fertility also the concept of immortality, an inestimable treasure. In ancient Babylon such treasure was protected by a serpent and the concept of two trees, the one of immortality attained through the heavily guarded one of wisdom, formed part of mythological belief. In biblical terms this is the tree of knowledge with the serpent that deprived Adam and Eve of paradise, and that became the central motif of a great number of nineteenth-century English samplers. In Scandinavia it is also a popular motif on samplers but is almost always disproportionately small in the general medley of patterns.

The regeneration of the tree, with its symbolism of spring, celebrated in Europe in hundreds of folk rites concerning the decoration of bushes or dancing round maypoles, surprisingly appears hardly at all in embroidery except in the maypole motif of Swedish samplers.

As the symbolism of fertility entwines the cult of the tree with that of the goddess, so the tree is also linked with hunting mythology. The palaeolithic hunters placed it at the cosmic centre and the shaman, emissary between the spirits of the animal world and their human hunters, still today ascends the cosmic tree on his journey of suffering and rebirth.

THE HUNT

Palaeolithic man was a hunter. He derived his food, clothing and even his shelter from the great herds that roamed shifting land masses between eras of glaciation and warming. As they were crucial to his survival he imbued the animals with souls, taking care as he killed them to ensure by magic rites their regeneration for his future needs. In the deep caves of northern Spain and southern France he drew symbols and abstractions of their shapes and powers. In the art of these sanctuaries of hunting magic animal is superimposed on animal with visible internal organs; a bovine with head turned is attacked by a predator; a shaman with stag's antlers takes on its identity as he dances.

Death for the primitive hunter was usually violent, understood to be the result of magic and not natural causes and therefore to be propitiated by ritual. His hunting terrain extended from Cantabria to Siberia and beyond to the Americas. After some thirty thousand years evidence of some of his hunting rituals are to be found in the embroidery of the same region from Spain to Siberia: the motif of the predator and hunted animal with body markings, the symbolism of horns representing the magic power of the animal itself, the role of the shaman, and the spiritual aspect of birds.

The steppelands, traditional home of the early nomadic hunters, extend from Asia to the Great Plain of Hungary and were always a transit region of eastward and westward migration bringing, for example, conquering peoples such as the Mongols into Europe. Shepherds of the Hungarian Plain wear embroidered skin and woollen coats, often with vestigial sleeves that indicate an Asian origin.

The predator and hunted animal

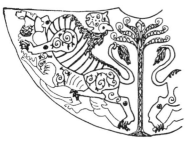

Palaeolithic decorative devices of hunted animal and predator, both with body markings, survive in the textiles of Pazyryk, the mantle of Sicily and the embroidery of Salamanca. The head was often separated by a collar and, in the case of the mantle, by the lion's claws.

The half turned head was another palaeolithic device that survives in embroidery, as in the indigo and white work of peasant China.

The most famous example in embroidery of the palaeolithic motif of a hunted animal attacked by a predator – in this case a camel and a lion – is on the coronation mantle of the Holy Roman Emperors, thought to have been made in Palermo in 1133–34 for Roger II of Sicily. Significantly, Sicily and Spain were the two points of penetration into Europe of Arab and thus oriental culture, and in Spain it is the embroidery of the small university town of Salamanca which features this palaeolithic design of the hunted animal, head half turned and separated from the body by a collar – a device also of Islamic art – with spaces in the body that originally represented the animal's organs. In these spaces the swastika, or symbols also worn as silver amulets such as the trout or heart, are worked. Over the head is normally a crown and in the mouth a curving floral branch. The animal may be either resting or rampant, and around it are flowing lines interspersed with flowers: the usual fertility symbols of carnations, tulips, pomegranates, but also lotus, papyrus and palms.

This motif of the hunted animal with curved head is used on certain Salamancan embroideries of ritual purpose, worked in pastel silks: cloths used as hangings for balconies and windows on the days of religious processions, as festival covers for chests, or as covers of gifts of bread and fruit on wedding days. The sleeves of women's linen bridal shirts, the neck and cuffs of men's, and also offertory cloths for the church, are embroidered with the same motifs but in black wool, with the small designs in the body spaces sometimes in red and blue.

Many of the felt saddle linings (*shabracks*) of Pazyryk, dating from about the fourth century BC, show the same hunted animal, with head turned and spaces in the body, attacked by a predator – usually a lion or eagle. The designs are appliquéd or inserted leather or felt, and the embroidery simply outlines them in cord, emphasizing the details in wool chain stitch. These animals in combat are usually winged and antlered and the spaces in their body are frequently depicted as punctuation marks. This style is typical of the animal art of the Scythians, kindred of the Pazyryk people.

In the embroideries of the Ioniàn islands of Greece the body spaces of stags and other animals are worked with smaller deer and birds. The same device of smaller versions of the creature within its own body features in the embroideries of the Paracas culture and lingers in the textiles of Guatemala.

The hunted animal with half-turned head is a frequent motif in one group of peasant embroideries of the isolated provinces of rural western China, mainly of Szechnan. Their indigo cotton thread patterning, that follows warp and weft and fills almost all the design areas leaving only a few elements in reserve, is in the tradition of the embroidery of the Miao tribes, spread across south-west China and northern Thailand. Mainly valances for the marriage bed, the embroideries are in cross stitch in indigo cotton thread on coarse white cotton with a pattern of medallions interspersed with small motifs.

Horned and antlered animals

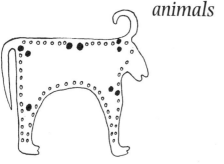

The talismanic power of horns is evident in the gold bovine plaque of Varna and the protective decoration of houses in Čičmany, Czechoslovakia, which is in turn reflected in the village embroidery.

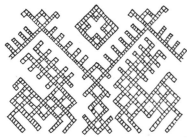

On Finnish and Russian embroidery antlers and deer are stylized almost beyond recognition, as on a headscarf from the Archangel district that formed part of the bride's dowry.

To primitive hunting societies the most important animals were horned and antlered. The curved horns of rams and goats had a myriad uses for the mounted nomads of the steppes and these animals were, after the horse, the most important element in their economy. The stag, deer, caribou and reindeer, too, formed the focus of human hunting economies and were worshipped not only for their meat and skins but also because the mystery of rebirth was manifest in the shedding and regrowth of their antlers. Elsewhere the buffalo, bison or bull were revered. Horns are still hung above doorways from Afghanistan to Spain as a protective device.

An early example of a horned animal used as a votive or amulet is the gold plaque of a bovine dating from 4500 BC, found in the tombs of Varna in Bulgaria. The holes in this plaque would indicate that it was stitched on to fabric.

Motifs derived from antlers and horns occur especially on embroidery from Central Asia, where they are also very common on carpets, felts and ikats, and from northern and Eastern Europe. North-American Indian hair embroidery also featured curved horn designs, until about 1860 when European-inspired floral designs took precedence. Though both derive from animals of the hunt antlers and horns as motifs diverge more and more with stylization, the antlers becoming almost lines of zigzags and the horns a double curve, even possibly a heart.

In Western European embroidery the stag itself as a motif features in depictions of the hunt and, having no particular symbolism, is portrayed naturalistically. Sibmacher's pattern book of 1597 contained a heavily antlered seated deer, which became a favourite motif on samplers.

Antlered animals

There are two aspects of antlered animals that relate to embroidery: the shape of antlers as a design motif and the use of the hair of the animal as thread.

Antlers as a motif are naturally found mainly in the embroidery of Siberia, northern Russia and Finland. Depiction is never realistic but always stylized, even into a pattern of mere interrelated zigzags. The linen shifts of the Siberian Mordu and Tcheremiss peoples bear such patterning over almost the entire surface, with white and blue or red beads, gold braiding, studs and sequins. In addition all the seams and the deep hem are appliquéd with red fabric. They were worn with headdresses which were often decorated with hanging bands of linen similarly appliquéd with red swastikas.

Hair embroidery was common to approximately two thirds of the northern world – the area between Scandinavia eastward to the Atlantic coast of Canada, where the reindeer of Europe and Asia and the caribou of America, both of the same *Rangifer* genus, and also moose, were indigenous. Hair embroidery probably originated during the period when reindeer were hunted rather than domesticated. In North America moose hair was preferred to caribou for embroidery and is often mistaken for quillwork, to which it bears a strong resemblance. In Siberia reindeer hair was most commonly used and is often combined with beadwork and paint. The finest work is that of the Aleuts who combined hair embroidery with fishskin and the gut of sea mammals. Only the Lapps have no tradition of hair embroidery, probably because of their early trade contacts with the Scandinavians, but edge their clothing with brightly coloured strips of wool and for embroidery use tin wrapped round sinew.

Much hair embroidery is endowed with magical properties. The hair chosen comes from the animal's throat and is white. The finest were sacred to some Siberian tribes and believed to impart magical force to the clothing of shamans. For the Montagnais Indians of north-eastern Canada mats of birchbark with caribou hair embroidery recorded the caribou killed by the owner and were reserved for important occasions, in particular for the *macusham*, a men's ceremonial feast associated with hunting magic.

Curved horns

Bovine horns as a motif, such as those of the ram, goat, buffalo, bison and bull, can be curved inward or outward, and often end in a spiral. The neolithic pots of China, for example, bear this pattern in both forms, combined with lunar and water symbolism. In embroidery, as in felts and carpets, this curved horn features particularly in the work of the peoples of Central Asia. It is also used as an amulet on the high embroidered hoods of the married tribal women of Kohistan. The height of the hood is determined by the number of sons the woman has borne, and if she is recognized in her village as something of a soothsayer a silver amulet symbolizing a ram's horns will be stitched on to the front of her hood.

The curved horn as a motif extends westward beyond the limits of the steppelands in the embroidery of the nomadic Sarakatsani of Greece. It is also found particularly on the embroidery of the homemade woollen garments of isolated sheep-rearing areas of Eastern Europe, where ancient motifs lingered. An example is the archaic rural clothing of the Yugoslav province of Montenegro, which contrasts with the entirely Turkish style of the costume of its capital Cetinje – before the First World War the town was a dazzling outpost of the Ottoman empire meriting a dozen or more opulent foreign embassies. At its westernmost point in the embroidery of Hungary and Bulgaria, the horn remains as a small hooked motif worked on the edge of patterns, usually in black thread.

When stylized, the curved horn motif with inwardly twisted spirals on prehistoric Chinese pots could be the basis of the heart pattern of Eastern and Central Europe. In the embroidery of Czechoslovakia a motif halfway between this design and the Western heart appears frequently. By the Alpine regions the heart as a sentimental motif is established and in folk art is naturalistically portrayed in the Western European manner, but still with the symbolic pomegranate, rose, carnation and tulip. The western-

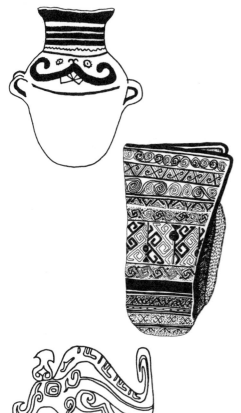

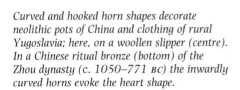

Curved and hooked horn shapes decorate neolithic pots of China and clothing of rural Yugoslavia; here, on a woollen slipper (centre). In a Chinese ritual bronze (bottom) of the Zhou dynasty (c. 1050–771 BC) the inwardly curved horns evoke the heart shape.

most geographical penetration of Asian peoples would seem to mark the region of transition from stylized inwardly curving horn to conventional heart.

Horned headdresses

Donning a horned headdress is still part of the shaman's ritual, putting him into contact with the spirit world: the dancing shaman with horned headdress in palaeolithic rock art is an image that has survived to the present day. Human heads with hair arranged in horn shapes, or with horned headdresses, feature on stone idols of the Russian steppelands dating from about 1000 BC; the Egyptian goddess of love, Hathor, is depicted in tomb paintings with a two-horned headdress holding the sundisc between the horns; the Sassanid kings of southern Iran wore single-horned caps which also, in a painting of the third century AD, supported the solar disc; Uygur women in the cave paintings of Chotso in Turfan, dating from the ninth to the tenth century AD, have a two-horned hairstyle; when the Spanish arrived in Mexico they drew pictures of the local women with their hair arranged in two horns; and this ancient concept survives to this day in the embroidered caps of Slovakia.

In the valley of the upper Hron river a string of villages, each with its own dialect though only a few miles apart, has retained its distinctive headdress, although the tradition would now seem to be slowly dying. Each village has a different style of cap, either one- or two-horned, beneath which the hair is first arranged in a complicated system of winding. In many places a ritual was associated with gathering a branch to make the wooden frame which often supplemented the hair. Women working in the fields wear their cap covered with a black scarf, which they remove to go to church or for special occasions. The old women of the Hron valley expect to be laid to rest in their best embroidered clothes and their cap, but now fear that by the time they die there will be no one left able to dress their hair so that they can be buried in their cap, whose horn symbolism links them to the spirit world.

Horned headdresses were common in Russia and in Bulgaria, Rumania, Transylvania and Albania. In Russia they were worn by the poorest peasants. Martha Wilmot, on her travels in the region in the early nineteenth century, comments that the mother of the nine-year-old girl she was given as a serf wore a kerchief and was thus a degree above the lowest peasants, who wore horned headdresses. In Moldavia women always had to wear a horned headdress to go to church and also to grind corn and bake consecrated bread for the sacrament.

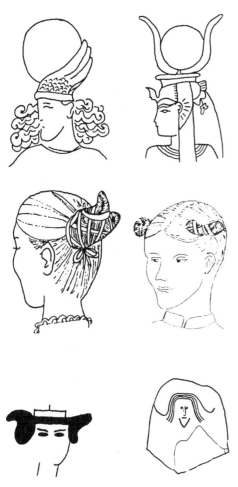

Origins of the single-horned headdress and hair arrangement can be seen in the Sassanid kings and of the double in the goddess Hathor. Double-horned hair arrangements are also found in cave paintings of Uygur women of the tenth century and on stone idols of the steppes dating from around 1000 BC.

Shamanism

The prime example of decoration endowing the wearer with the magical force of the creature it symbolizes is the shaman. Originating in the hunting societies of the palaeolithic era, shamanism lingers in the Arctic north, Korea, pockets of South-East Asia, Aboriginal Australia, Africa, among the Ainu and American Indian tribes and in South America. Everything in the natural world has a spirit which the shaman controls.

The shaman is identified by his costume and its decoration. The wearing of antlers to associate him with the animal world and invest him with its powers and spirits is common, as is the hanging on his vestments of all manner of symbolic accoutrements: amulets which in Islamic countries contain Koranic verses, bells to arouse the soul, trophies of the hunt, towels with stylized antler motifs embroidered in red. The embroidered decoration on his clothing is in sacred white reindeer thread and is often of skeletal patterning – ribs and bones – symbolizing his figurative death and subsequent rebirth.

Mystical animals found in archaic embroidery are those linked with shamanism such as the jaguar, an animal who hunts at night and who in the Americas was the shaman's familiar. The bear in many northern cultures was believed to be a human ancestor and guardian. It was revered by the Ainu, whose appliqué patterns portray the bear, and by the Giliak of Siberia. For their festival, when the men of one clan about to marry into another are invited to kill the bear, clothing is worn with embroidered spiral patterns that symbolize the animal. Stags, like birds, were believed to transport souls between earth and heaven: most shamanistic ritual is accompanied by the use of hallucinogenics, especially magic mushrooms, and a state of transcendence, or trance, was linked to the stag. Creatures believed by some peoples to be incarnations of the soul, such as lizards or toads or bees and particularly birds, were also mystical.

Birds

Birds almost everywhere represent the spirit world. They are messengers from heaven, the sky and the sun gods, and they carry the souls of the departed to the afterlife, where they become birds themselves. The Ugrians of Siberia tattoo birds on their shoulders to keep the soul in the body, carve them on cradles to prevent offspring wandering in the woods during sleep, and embroider them on fishskin bridal robes as symbols of the souls that would lodge in the future children.

In South-East Asia, too, spirits of the dead were believed to take the form of birds. Thus people with birds' heads are a motif found on the ritual sarongs of the women of Lampung in Sumatra, appearing as figures on the ships of the dead patterns that are the main feature of one type of these embroideries. In Borneo the hornbill was venerated and features in simple embroidery on barkcloth coats and festive hangings.

Birds are one of the most common embroidery motifs in the world, often associated with the tree of life, with solar patterns and with floral symbols of fertility. They may range from a simple good luck symbol to a statement of spiritual belief that is shared by a clan but remains ultimately private and personal, such as the thunderbird of American Indian tribes. The thunderbird, generally accepted as a benign creature of the upper world, bringing rain and fertility, but who also attacked the evil animal life of the

The traditional symbol of the Ghiliak Siberian bride is the tree of life carrying birds that represent the children to be born.

The angels of a Russian altar frontal of 1389 betray their origin as birds.

underworld with lightning, is decoratively transposed as the thunderbird pattern combined with zigzags.

Birds as an ornamental motif are chosen for their general symbolism, or else for the specific attributes of their species – power, epitomized by the eagle and condor, the regal beauty of the peacock, or such harbingers of daylight as the cock. The latter, believed to chase away the evil spirits of the night, is often associated with solar symbolism and with the tree of life, for the rebirth of the day mirrors the rebirth of the seasons. Most commonly the cock is depicted in confronting pairs with or without a centrally placed related symbol.

In Christianity the symbolic attributes of birds as messengers from heaven are assumed by angels and in many embroideries these are little but birds in disguise.

THE SUN
Origins of the cult

Of the conventional pictographs for the sun the Bouriate people of Siberia take the crossed disc and combine it with the moon, the tree of life and symbols of shamanism on a cult drawing.

In a small quiet garden of ancient Carthage, now an affluent suburb of Tunis, broken stone stelae lie around a sacrificial altar where first-born sons were beheaded to honour the sun god Ba'al Hammon and the fertility goddess Tanit. A sun demanding human blood was also a Mayan cult, whereas for another great sun-worshipping civilization, the ancient Egyptians, it was the beneficent and positive aspects that were venerated: its life-giving rays and daily rebirth. To palaeolithic hunting societies the sun was the greatest hunter of all, nightly slaying the stars but ensuring the survival of their souls so that they would return the next evening.

Primitive veneration of the sun did not always lead to formalized solar cults. It was almost always inextricably linked with that of the moon, which because of its waxing and waning, its control over tides and waters and its mystical relation to the menstrual cycle of women, held a stronger position in pagan mythology. In most societies the sun was regarded as male and the moon as female, though in some this was reversed. European languages, for example, still retain this duality.

The pictographs that conventionally denote the sun in decorative arts, and that are found in embroidery over most of the world, already appear in palaeolithic art. Concentric circles were originally a lunar symbol and with the addition of a cross became solar; the simple circle with a cross is also solar and conveys the linking of the four corners of the earth. The spiral, as well as expressing creative force, symbolizes the sun and the moon and was especially important in Bronze-Age Scandinavia and in Celtic and Viking traditions. The circle with a central dot, the whorl with twisted rays and the circle with straight rays all feature in cave paintings.

The swastika, another accepted solar symbol, but more complex in that it also expresses concepts of movement and change, first appears in the neolithic period around 4000 BC, together with the rosette as a solar emblem. A rosette is also formed by the opened petals of the lotus, a flower associated with the sun, especially in Egyptian and Hindu mythology.

continued on page 105

HE GREAT GODDESS

4   Marriage coif, Bekalta, Tunisia. The
zenge shape of the three goddess figures on
his marriage coif recalls that of the
rehistoric figurine of Venus found at
espugue. The raised arms are a ritual stance
ken by the Tunisian bride at her marriage
lwa when she is presented to her guests
earing such a coif. The fish and sun are
ccompanying symbols.

5   Ritual towel, Russia. Russian towels,
eremoniously hung over birch trees or at
rossroads, abound with depictions of the
arth goddess, almost always embroidered
ntirely in red. Most show her in various
tages of transmutation into plant form, and
vith her arms raised. Accompanying birds,
-pointed stars, swastikas, zigzags and
lternating pattern make her identity clear.

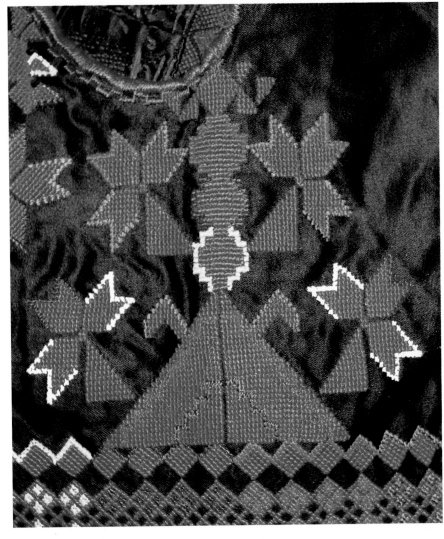

66 Left: *Woman's marriage shift, Attica, Greece. Marriage shifts show a more obvious fertility goddess than the everyday ones, repeatedly enclosed in a somewhat phallic shape. The embroidery was usually the work of professional women, with different women having responsibility for coloured silk or goldwork.*

67 Above: *Picture, England (1930s). The motifs of 1930s English embroidery sprang from nostalgia for a vanishing rural life, but the crinoline lady herself was an anachronism. Holding a bunch of flowers, might she not also perhaps derive, through more obvious examples in the peasant embroidery then being copied, from the goddess holding her sacred branch?*

68 *Mola, Kuna Blas Indian, Panama. The theme of many molas is obscure. Lizard-like creatures and upraised arms are associated with the goddess, while the mouth bristling with teeth symbolizes in the art of the Americas the concept of death as part of life. Four strips refer to stages of the eight-layered heaven and underworld of Kuna mythology.*

69 *Woman's dress, Saraqib, Syria, depicting the goddess with upraised arms. Ancient Syrian association with goddess worship is evident in Phoenician cult and is reflected in the thirteenth-century pottery of Raqqa and Hama where the goddess is a decorative device.*

73 Opposite: *Skirt hem, Crete. In her European guise as a mermaid the primitive goddess with splayed legs came through Renaissance pattern into the embroidery of Crete, both on women's skirts and ecclesiastical robes. She is still flanked by birds.*

70 Top left: *Roman mosaic, second century AD, Tunisia. The stance of the goddess with outspread legs is found in almost all primitive art and came into European iconography as a two-tailed mermaid, often with a masculine face.*

71 Cloth, India. *The goddess is still discernible as a two-tailed mermaid and is flanked by birds. The animal life that denoted her fertility became in later art her acolytes.*

72 Cloth, Ionian Islands, Greece. *The goddess figure, with animals and plants arranged in an orderly fashion around her, is found on archaic Greek vases. With wings as well as arms, this goddess resembles votive figurines of the third millennium BC from the Cyclades. The flowers with her are the usual tulip and carnation, symbols of fertility.*

74 Ritual towel, Russia. The goddess raises her arms and the flat-topped shape of her head is reminiscent of Minoan goddess figurines. The horseman recalls the one approaching the goddess on the great felt of Pazyryk dating from about the fifth century BC.

75 Sampler, England, mid-seventeenth century. A derivation of a worshipper offering a sacred branch appears on seventeenth-century English samplers as the 'boxer' motif. The goddess is usually transmuted into a plant of obvious anthropomorphic aspect.

76 Ritual towel, Russia. Water, as part of the birth process and therefore of cosmic creation, is associated with the goddess. The ship of life sailing through the cosmic waters is one of her attributes and a common embroidery motif.

77 Sampler, England, mid-seventeenth century. Mermaids, as guardians of the cosmic waters, often with mirror in hand, are a motif of seventeenth-century English samplers.

78　Towel border, Turkey. Symbols expressing the fertility of the goddess are commonplace. The tulip, resembling the female vulva, and the pomegranate with its blood-red seeds, are obvious ones. The cypress in Phoenician lore represented the tree of life

79　Bedding cover, Uzbek Lakai, Afghanistan. The carnation is very frequently embroidered together with the pomegranate or tulip to symbolize fertility, and the cross is also a manifestation of the tree of life.

80　Towel, Russia. Ritual towels showing the goddess were sometimes replaced in the nineteenth century with towels of modern figures but still with the fertility symbols of the pomegranate and carnation and with flanking animals.

THE TREE OF LIFE

1   Cloth, Ottoman, probably Balkan. The
tree of life transposed as a vase containing
flowers or a plant was a device of Sumerian
art. The flowers were usually those
associated with fertility, and the tree was
still flanked by birds and figures. It is here
supplemented with large pomegranates. This
piece recalls the nakshe of Azerbaijan in its
version of the tree of life, the suzanis of
Tashkent, the archaic patterns of Samokov in
Bulgaria in its pomegranates and the skirt
hems of Crete in the style of its linear
embroidery.

2   Purse, Afghanistan. The tree of life in
its various guises is one of the most common
motifs in embroidery almost everywhere.
Reduced to its simplest form it protects the
contents of this purse. One piece of mirror
strategically placed, jazzy colours and tassels
also play a role.

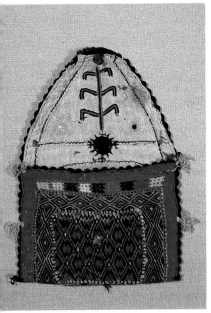

83 Marriage shawl, El Jem, Tunisia. The archaic patterns on the woollen marriage shawls of El Jem, Sfax and Ksour Esaf in Tunisia depict the tree of life with guardian serpents and with solar symbols, motifs believed to protect the bride from evil spirits.

84 Coverlet, Castelo Branco, Portugal. Coverlets were made in this small town from the early seventeenth century, when Portugal was still active in India, until the end of the nineteenth century when a disease of silkworms brought the tradition to an end. Many depict the tree of life, as in Indian palampores, rising out of a hillock, with symbolic pomegranates, carnations and small birds.

85 Marriage headcloth, Patzún, Guatemala. Trees were linked to the magic power of crossroads and the cross is one aspect of the tree at the centre of the universe. Flanking birds and animals betray this Guatemalan motif as an import from another culture.

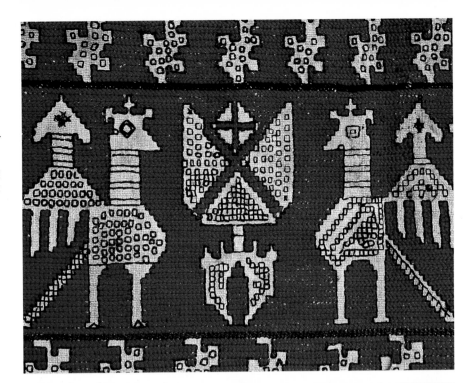

86 *Cloth, Azemmour, Morocco. From a base of carnations the tree of life is pared down to a simple stylized carnation alternating with another version as a column, both flanked by birds.*

87 *Ritual cloth, Russia. In its fertile fruit-bearing aspect the tree of life often bore a goddess in its branches. Symbolic motifs of two-headed eagles and cocks, carnations and further goddesses surround the tree while at its core is a heart, itself probably derived from horn symbolism.*

88 *Cushion for marriage sleigh, Sweden. The tree symbolizing the goddess was often flanked by worshippers or by birds or animals, which could vary locally. The horse was an object of pre-Christian cult and was both a solar and lunar symbol.*

89 *Woman's bonnet, Rybany, Slovakia. The heart as part of the tree of life, with the symbolic pomegranate and confronting birds, is worked in wool or heavy silk on the bonnets and blouses of Rybany. A solar rosette sometimes replaces the heart.*

90 *Woman's blouse, Djerba, Tunisia. The motif of the tree transposed as a vase containing a plant or flowers, especially carnations, and still with flanking birds, was disseminated by the pattern books of Europe. It became the favourite motif of the folk art of Europe, spreading from there to the Middle East and North Africa.*

91 *Woman's dress, Ramallah, Palestine. The tree of life as a vase of flowers flanked by birds was among patterns from European books introduced in Ramallah from the late nineteenth century when Quakers founded schools there and promoted embroidery. The traditional motifs of Palestinian embroidery were geometric.*

92 Woman's dress, Kaulan, Yemen. The cosmic tree of primitive mythology was sometimes conceived as an inverted image, drawing strength through its roots in heaven and bestowing them on the world. This is frequently depicted as the central trunk with radiating lines of a pine or palm tree, or as an upside-down vase.

93 Sampler, England (1826). The biblical tree of knowledge is the central motif of many nineteenth-century English samplers, and is shown in a more natural rendering, but still with flanking birds and animals and also carnations.

4 Cover, Salamanca, Spain. The palaeolithic design of a hunted animal, head half turned and separated from the body by a collar – a device also of Islamic art – features in the embroideries of the town of Salamanca in Spain. The motif is often combined with trout and with the swastika, both symbols also worn as silver amulets. The designs were worked in black wool on linen shifts and in pastel silks on ritual cloths.

5 Shepherd's coat, Nuristan, Afghanistan. The ubiquitous horn motifs of the carpets and felts of Central Asia, as also of the embroideries, decorate in a random fashion the heavy wool coats of the shepherds of Nuristan. The patterns are combined with solar whorls. Horned animals were essential to the economy of the peoples of Asia and horns are still placed above doorways as a protective device.

96 Woman's hood, Kohistan, Pakistan. A tribal woman of Kohistan who is recognized as something of a soothsayer in her village has a silver amulet symbolizing a ram's horns sewn on to the front of her hood. The height of the hood is determined by the number of sons she has borne.

97 Girl's bolero, Luhacovice, Moravia. The curved horn motif with inwardly twisted spirals, found on prehistoric Chinese pots, could be the basis of the heart pattern of Eastern and Central Europe. It appears frequently in the embroideries of Czechoslovakia in this form, but by the Alpine regions of Western Europe the pattern is a conventional heart.

98 Woman's bonnet, Polomka, Slovakia. The ancient horned headdress, augmented by dressing the hair in a single or double horn or using a wooden frame to support it, survived in Eastern Europe and is still found in the bonnets of the married women of the Hron valley in Slovakia. Some headdresses are of the single horned shape, as those of Polomka, and some double as those of Rousse in Bulgaria.

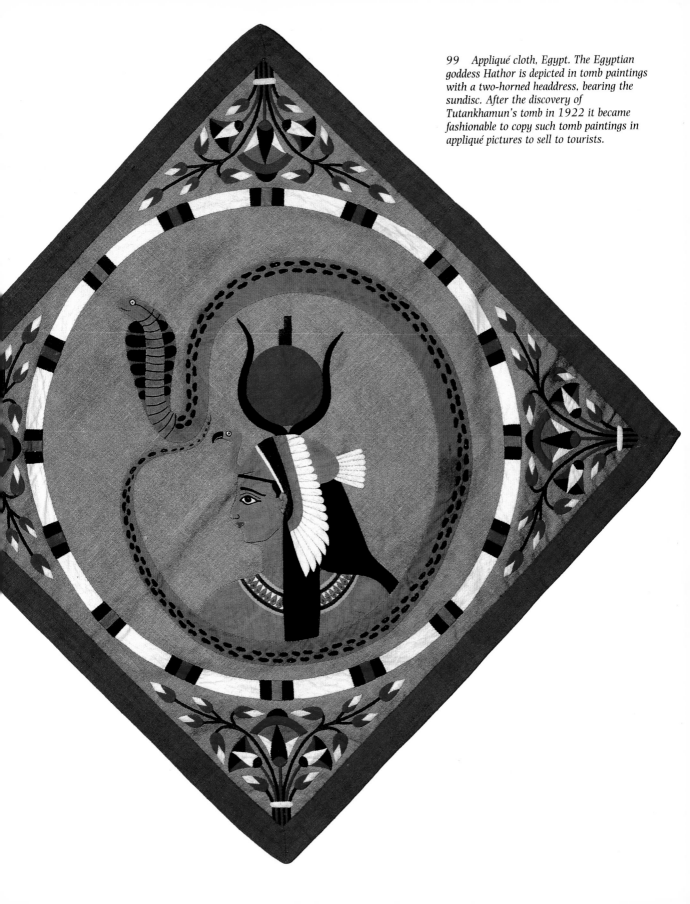

99 Appliqué cloth, Egypt. The Egyptian goddess Hathor is depicted in tomb paintings with a two-horned headdress, bearing the sundisc. After the discovery of Tutankhamun's tomb in 1922 it became fashionable to copy such tomb paintings in appliqué pictures to sell to tourists.

100 War coat, Asante, Ghana. Talismanic charms sewn on to clothing were used by hunters, warriors and also shamans. The shaman, originating in the hunting societies of the palaeolithic era, also identifies himself with the animal world by decoration. For the hunter the amulets afford protection.

101 Hem of leggings, Ainu people, Japan. To the Ainu of Japan the bear was the shaman's familiar and believed to be a human ancestor and guardian. He is stylized into a pattern on the edges of their clothing.

102 Pouch, Ojibwa or Ottowa, N. America. Thunderbirds were mythological beings that caused thunder and lightning and brought the spring rains. As air spirits they fought against underwater deities such as panthers. In embroidery they are often depicted with zigzag patterning denoting lightning.

103 Opposite: Door hangings, sakhyo, toran, Kanebi caste, Kutch, India. Birds are often chosen as symbols of the attributes of their species. The peacock is not only a bird of regal beauty but is also associated with sun worship and is an emblem of Sarasvati, Hindu goddess of wisdom, music and poetry. Hangings such as these decorate doorways in India on special occasions.

THE SUN

104 Above: *Doorway, Benares, India. Many protective devices, such as horns, fish hands, crosses, diamonds, rosettes and swastikas are carved or painted on buildings in many parts of the world, especially over doorways. Solar mythology is one source of such protection.*

105 *Marriage dress, Siwa oasis, Egypt. The black and white marriage dresses of the Siwa oasis are embroidered with a sunburst design over the entire front. Lines of chain stitch from seven blocks of pattern at the neck are interspersed with solar symbols and buttons of white pearl or coloured plastic.*

106 *Marriage shawl, Ksour Esaf, Tunisia. Marriage shawls add the sun and crescent moon to the tree of life and strange anthropomorphic patterns, believed to protec the bride from evil spirits.*

107 Opposite: *Sampler, Mexico. Solar mythology was linked with the moon. In European style embroidery the sun and moo together, especially with the crucifix and Catholic symbols such as IHS, more frequently convey the darkening of the sky a Christ's death, recounted by Luke.*

108 *Cloth, Buzsák, Hungary. In European embroidery, motifs derived from the sun are mainly in the form of rosettes. In the village of Buzsák, near Lake Balaton, such rosette patterns are combined with hooked spirals. The spiral is an associated solar symbol and also expresses creative force.*

109 *Shift sleeve, Samokov, Bulgaria. The sleeves of women's linen shifts of the small Bulgarian towns of Samokov and Stanke Dimitrov are embroidered with a solar motif combined with spirals. They also always feature a comb-like pattern: such a pattern on early Paracas textiles denoted rain.*

110 *Suzani, Tashkent, Uzbekistan. Though suzanis are regarded as floral embroideries, the 'flower heads' on those of Tashkent, as this one, are large plain red discs of solar aspect, while the suzanis of Pskent are overtly solar, with astrological patterns of suns, moons, stars and solar symbols.*

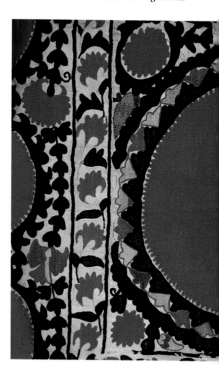

11 Cloth, Uzbek Lakai, Afghanistan. Many tent hangings, bedding covers and dowry cloths of the Uzbek Lakai are embroidered with the solar symbol of a freewheeling whorl. On this cloth this pattern is combined with motifs of heart-shaped aspect which enclose tulips, symbol of fertility.

112 Above: *Wedding canopy, Rajasthan, India. Canopies erected at weddings in Rajasthan have a solar disc as the central motif. Variations of this are the central lotus itself also a solar symbol, on the canopies of Gujarat, and also on the kanthas of Bengal.*

113 *Woman's dress, Kohistan, Pakistan. The solar discs embroidered on the women's dresses and blouses and children's jackets of Kohistan resemble the patterns carved on rocks from the fifth millennium BC onwards along the route of the nearby Karakorum highway. There was once a flourishing sun cult in the region. These patterns are always outlined in white beads and have added buttons, coins and metal discs.*

114 *Woman's skirt, Bansali caste, Kutch, India. The Bansalis, a Hindu farming caste, believe themselves descended from the sun god Surya and the women wear yellow or orange skirts embroidered with sun discs.*

The four-rayed star served as a symbolic representation of Shamash, the Sumerian sungod, and later became the Maltese cross, while the 8-pointed star, one of the most common motifs of all in embroidery, represented his consort Gula.

The axe was a solar emblem of the sky gods and an Egyptian solar symbol. The double axe possibly conveyed the union of the sky gods with the earth goddess and was imbued with magic power by people as diverse as the Yoruba of West Africa and the Minoans of Crete. There are many possible interpretations of its meaning and derivation; it is believed to represent, for example, the wings of the goddess, and the waxing and waning of the moon, but it is always associated with fertility.

Solar worship is manifested in embroidery in varied ways in different regions of the world:

North Africa
Egypt The embroideries of Egypt that seem to be intimately linked with the cult of the sun are those of the Siwa oasis in the western desert. Amid the date palms and olive groves of this large oasis, once an important staging post on the only route across a waterless desert, are ancient solar temples. The area is populated by the original Berber and Bedouin, who still retain their own languages, and were known as worshippers of the sun god Amon-Ra.

Siwan girls are married at about fourteen and the family of the bride sew all the clothes. For their wedding, and for the only other occasions on which they stepped out of their homes – to go to other marriages and funerals and to congratulate a new mother on the birth of her child – women wore seven underdresses: white, red, then silk ones of black, yellow, blue, orange and green and on top the embroidered wedding dress, either of white or black.

This overdress is cut wide with deep sleeves and is embroidered with a sunburst pattern over the entire front. Rows of chain stitch around the neck and front opening, often also seven in number, are edged with seven blocks of almost solid embroidery, three on each side and one at the centre front, sometimes finished with multicoloured ties with tassels. From these emanate lines of fine stitchery interspersed with small patterns, mainly also solar symbols: Maltese crosses, small stars, spinning circles, double axes. At each corner of the blocks and down the neck opening are white pearl buttons, though on some the entire front is decorated with buttons, often in groups of three which in other cultures, such as the Naga of Assam, denotes a star. The dominant colours of yellow, orange and red are also solar. Sometimes green, blue and black are added, which with the white pearl buttons make the seven colours of Siwan embroidery. These same colours, with purple instead of black, are the seven colours of joy associated with the sun in Sindhi embroidery. In modern work coloured plastic buttons replace the pearl ones, but the colour range is normally adhered to. Similar embroidery decorates the headscarf and trousers worn with the dresses.

Egyptian appliqué pictures of the goddess Hathor with the sundisc between her horns are not designs that still remain from ancient sun worship, but are merely copies of tomb paintings that it became fashionable to make and sell to tourists after the discovery of Tutankhamun's tomb.

Tunisia The coastal plain of Tunisia is planted with soldierly rows of olive trees from which rises, like the cathedral of Chartres above the cornfields of Beauce, the Roman amphitheatre of the small town of El Jem, sixth biggest of the Roman world. The bride of El Jem, and of the large village of Ksour Esaf not far distant – a poor place of narrow unmade streets and adobe buildings – wears seven white tunics, a jacket and a hood all heavily worked with gold, and with them a headshawl of either indigo or henna-dyed wool, embroidered with archaic motifs. The origin of most of these motifs, which can be either plant-like, reptilian or anthropomorphic, is impossible to determine, but there is no ambiguity in the depiction of the sun and moon. The embroidery forms a wide band along the edge worn over the forehead, and is in thick couched threads, beneath which a line of tassels frames the face. These bridal textiles were a present from mother to daughter.

The Americas

Many North American tribes considered the sun to be the god of creation and made sacrificial offerings to it. Symbols of the sun are a widespread motif in the embroidery and tattooing of the Iroquois and Algonquin.

Central and South America The solar worship of the Aztecs, the Incas and Mayans has left little trace in embroidery, though in the brocaded weavings of Guatemala and Bolivia the sun is a common motif, stylized into a diamond shape. In embroidery pre-Conquest cloaks of Mexico were decorated with designs of solar rays but once subject to European influence, the sun motif appears infrequently, and then depicted with the moon and Catholic symbols.

It is particularly in the men's black suits of the Guatemalan town of Santo Tomás Chichicastenango that the ancient sun motifs survive. A flap, usually called an ear, made of light-coloured cotton, is attached to the side of the trouser leg, extending from hip to knee. On it are embroidered solar patterns which indicate the age and virility of the wearer. The most ornate, known as the *Ma Kij* – or *Abuelo Sol*, 'grandfather sun' in Spanish – has a large rayed sun with extra flowers and leaves, and is worn by virile men between twenty-five and sixty. A man who is sterile does not have the right to wear this decoration. From puberty to the age of twenty-five the pattern is of two plainer suns, one below the other. The upper one represents the elder man who still takes precedence over the younger. From the age of

At the procession of All Souls' Night in Chichicastenango, the men wear their solar-embroidered costumes and carry images of Santo Tomás and of the sun. Fireworks are let off only after magicians have been consulted.

about six a boy has one simple rayed sun, with a cross below it to which rays will be added as he reaches puberty.

The short black woollen jacket worn with these trousers has a sun embroidered in chain stitch at the base of the neck opening. The costume was worn every day until about the 1930s but is now only used for festive occasions. The work is done by men embroiderers of the town and motifs of flowers and birds are gradually supplanting the symbolic suns.

Europe

In European embroidery motifs derived from the sun are mainly in the form of rosettes, though the ritual towels of Russia associated with the goddess depict the sun as a galloping horse, recalling its trajectory across the sky, or as a magnificent firebird, in honour of the marvel of its appearing in spring at the end of a long dark winter. The sunbird was already a solar symbol in the palaeolithic era.

In Brittany the motif known as 'the peacock's feather' on the embroidered jackets of Pont-Aven comes from an Indo-European symbol first found in the rock drawings of Bohusland and in the fibulae and bronze knives of prehistoric Denmark. It represents the sun, or more especially the ship of the sun. These embroideries are always in yellow or orange, colours with obvious solar associations.

In Spain the village of Lagartera in the province of Toledo is still the commercial centre for embroidery. Here the women's linen blouses, *gorgueras*, which cover the chest and back and tie under the arms with tape, have a dominant front border of spirals. Instead of the satin and back stitch of the rest of the embroidery the spirals are worked in a double loop stitch known as '*punto real*', giving a raised effect. Edging these, and worked round the neck and outer edges, are repeated motifs of the tree of life, confronting birds or animals and stylized carnations. All the embroidery is in black wool and the fabric is homespun handwoven linen. Similar blouses from the nearby village of Navalcan have patterns based on the labyrinth instead of the spiral.

In Eastern Europe solar patterns are mostly Central Asian in origin. They are frequently worked in wool or in leather appliqué and are combined with associated symbols such as hooked spirals and birds. The rosette is the most common form and there are many examples in the embroidery of Hungary and of Slovakia. In Buzsák, close to Lake Balaton in Hungary, for instance, the women embroider cloths in black and red with circles and rosettes combined with hooked spirals, while in the village of Rybany in Slovakia the women work a rosette flanked by birds and tulips on the back of their linen caps and across the sleeves of their shifts.

Solar-derived motifs in the embroidery of Bulgaria and Yugoslavia are more obviously pagan. In Bulgaria the sleeves of the linen shifts of Samokov and Stanke Dimitrov, small mountain towns to the south of Sofia, are embroidered with a solar motif with rays ordered into a comb-

The 'peacock feather' pattern of men's and women's jackets of Finistère, Brittany, derives from prehistoric solar motifs. The bands of patterning never vary, but are more richly embroidered on the side front worn outside for festivities and inside for mourning.

The solar motif of a quadruple hook, derived from the swastika, is embroidered in chain stitch on woollen fabric, grada, and appliquéd at the hip of a Serbian woman's woollen jacket, sadak.

like row and combined with spirals. The same comb-like pattern on Paracas textiles denoted rain. In Yugoslavia spirals and swastikas on the sleeveless woollen coats of Serbia, Croatia and Montenegro evolve into a four-hooked pattern incorporating associated symbols of horns, stars, triangles, zigzags and S-shapes. These patterns are worked in chain stitch on pieces of homespun wool of red, blue or green which are then applied to the garment.

Central Asia

Portable wealth in the form of textiles is part of the nomadic way of life of the peoples who wander across the steppelands of Central Asia and who are only now adopting a more settled way of life. Of the greatest importance were felts and carpets, embroideries less so. All have solar motifs, which can be circular, as discs and whorls, or a circle within a circle (a pattern used in felts and believed to ward off the evil eye) or versions of the scroll motif known as 'running dog' or 'wave'. This reversible pattern was presumed mystic as it bears the magical significance of the balance between life and death, light and dark, male and female, sun and moon. It is a pattern also found on neolithic pottery of Old Europe.

Pazyryk textiles featured the mystic patterns of a row of horns and the 'running dog' scroll motif associated with the sun and moon.

The most famous embroideries are the *suzanis* made by the Uzbek, a mixture of peoples who grouped under Uzbek Khan when he conquered the central steppelands in the early fourteenth century. They are large hangings or bedcovers worked as dowry pieces and made in the area from Bokhara and Nurata in the west to Tashkent and Pskent in the east.

They are made of strips of unbleached cotton or linen embroidered predominantly in reds and pinks, with touches of contrasting colour, in Bokhara or Roumanian couching, with some chain stitch. Most are floral with the field of flower motifs divided by stems and leaves into latticework. Further east the source of their pattern is more solar than floral. In the *suzanis* of Tashkent the flowers become large plain red discs and cover the field almost entirely, the leaves and stems reduced to small tendrils. In Pskent the designs are overtly solar, with astrological patterns of suns, moons, stars and solar symbols.

During the early twentieth century many Uzbeks left Russia for Afghanistan where they could still lead a nomadic life. Among them was a particularly wild and tough group of mounted warriors, the Lakai. The embroidered dresses of their women and the small mats for wrapping presents that girls made for their dowry have solar motifs in the form of whorls, together with rams' horns, hook and wave patterns, spirals and stars. Similar motifs of freewheeling whorls and discs, horns, spirals and circles, and also fish and exotic unrecognizable plant forms, are very common on the embroidery of the Kalmuk, a people who live to the north of the Caucasus mountains.

Another brigandly tribe were the Tekke Türkmen, who were known for their raids into Persia stealing women and even men. O'Donovan, visiting the Merv oasis in 1880, described these people as ruffianly, irreclaimable scamps who, when they rode into town, were made to leave their swords and guns with the guard at the town gate and allowed only their knives. The embroidery of the women of the tribe features repeat swastikas on the cuffs of the trousers they make for their dowry, in the same interlaced stitch with ridged outline called *kesdi* in which they work the tulip and hook motifs of their cloaks.

India and Pakistan

The high mountain passes through the Hindu Kush, the Pamirs and Karakorum, though in modern times obstructed by national frontiers, were an established route from the deserts traversed by the silk roads to the Indus valley and Indian subcontinent. The recent construction of the Karakorum highway, blasting a path through wild terrain, has disclosed petroglyphs carved on rocks along its way from the fifth millennium BC onwards.

The earliest are of palaeolithic hunting magic. Later animals of the first millennium BC show the same characteristics as the animals of Scythian art. As Buddhism spread through the first and second centuries pictorial Buddhist themes were incised alongside and over the ancient designs. By the ninth and tenth centuries there seems to have been a revolt against Buddhism. Roughly hewn motifs appear of axes, mounted worshippers or deities and especially of sun discs. Not only had sun worship been brought to this area many centuries before by migrating peoples from the west bringing the Phoenician sun god Ba'al, the Greek Helios and the Sumerian Shamash, but also at the period the rock carvings were made there was a flourishing sun cult in Kashmir and at Multan in the steppelands, whose sun temple was the main sanctuary for the whole region.

Kohistan In Kohistan – the region bordering the valley where the highway passes – embroidery motifs on the women's and children's clothing resemble the solar emblems on the rock carvings, either in the form of eight rays within a squared-off disc, or more usually, a disc divided into sections.

The motifs cover the deep sleeves and bodice fronts of the women's black cotton dresses, their short flared skirts made of hundreds of godets being left plain. Usually a particularly complex disc is set at the shoulders. One also forms the centrepiece of the V-shaped back flap of the women's hoods. They are also worked on blouses and children's jackets.

The embroidery is in floss silk thread in darning stitch forming narrow diagonal rows with voiding between, with some finely worked detailing in cross stitch, especially on garment edges. The predominant colour is ruby red, with touches of yellow, orange and green. All motifs are outlined with small white beads and accentuated by white buttons, and the garments themselves are lined with floral print or blue cotton and bordered with lead beads or old zips.

Swat Close by in the valley of the river Swat which rises in these mountains

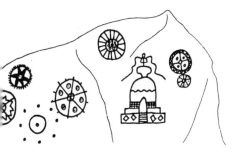

Boulders along the Karakorum highway have been carved through the centuries with solar discs, hunting scenes, horsemen, figures, animals, axes and Buddhist stūpas.

the women embroider their black cotton dresses over the entire front. shoulders and cuffs with diamond-shaped rather than circular discs, and with a proliferation of horned motifs. The work is in shocking pink floss silk in darning stitch, mainly arranged in diagonal rows with voiding, and is outlined in yellow double running, with touches of green and white.

Sind The greatest of the rivers whose source lies in these mountains is the Indus, home at Harappa and Mohenjo-daro of one of mankind's earliest civilizations. In its lower reaches in the province of Sind are to be found groups of tombs built from the fifteenth century on, the major ones sited in the desert at Chaukhandi. The tombs are ornately carved in sections, some with geometric motifs and some with rosettes symbolizing the sun, sometimes cut in half as though rising or setting. The men's tombs are often capped with a carved turban, a custom also of Turkey where a man's turban is placed on an indoor tomb and preserved as an effigy. The women's are decorated with the pattern of their necklace and earrings.

The people of Sind have retained many of their ancient animistic beliefs and the patterns on these tombs are still worked on the women's embroidery, especially that of the Lohana merchant class and the Jats, herders who are believed to have originated in the region of Iran/Iraq. The fronts of their backless blouses, *choli*, are worked in sections with rosettes, some halved, interspersed with geometric pattern. The whole bodice is dominated by mirrorwork which forms the centres of the rosettes and defines the remaining pattern areas.

Gujarat Many of the same peoples, Hindu and Muslim herders and farmers, straddle the political border of Pakistan and India. Those in Gujarat retain from the ancient Indian belief in the sun god Surya the symbol of a circle or swastika on their embroideries. In particular the Kanebi Hindu farmers embroider sun discs together with swastikas, dancing women and peacocks on their skirts and on the borders of their *sadlo*, a draped shawl given to women at the end of their first year of marriage. The Kanebi combine interlacing stitch in white cotton with open chain in yellow, green and pink.

The Bansalis, another Hindu farming group from the Kutch area of Gujarat, believe they are descended from Surya and the women wear skirts covered with sun circles embroidered in running stitch on yellow or orange cotton fabric.

The desert tombs of Sind are carved with rosette patterns symbolizing the sun and closely resembling the mirrorwork blouses of Sindhi women. Offerings to the spirits, in the form of bits of rag, hairs, or dead animals or their skins, are hung on the tombs or tied to the nearest bush.

3
RELIGION AND ITS PATTERNS

TAOISM

The world's major religions were all established in the thousand-year period between 500 BC and AD 500, with the exception of Islam which followed Muhammad's flight from Mecca to Medina in AD 622. Within these structured world religions the purpose of most embroidered textiles is to decorate churches, temples, mosques and synagogues. Such specifically ecclesiastical embroidery is not the concern of this book, but rather the patterns and influences that established religions have introduced into secular embroidery. Of all secular embroidery, by far the strongest influence of religious philosophy is on that of China, where Confucianism, Taoism and Buddhism existed together. Taoist beliefs in particular, and other symbols associated with Chinese religious thought, feature on most embroideries, even those made for export where such patterns are meaningless to the recipient.

The Taoists, originally alchemists, loosely followed the teachings of Lao-Tse, a philosopher believed to have lived in about the fifth century BC. Their priests' robes are richly embroidered with motifs which include the *yin/yang* (female/male) principle of the universe, surrounded by the eight trigrams, the mystic complex of three broken and unbroken lines which is also a motif on secular costume.

The eight holy men of Taoism are known as 'Immortals' as they had the right to feast on the fruit of immortality at the peach festival of Hsi Wang Mu, the goddess who ruled over a fairy realm in Western Paradise. Each is associated with an attribute which commonly stands alone, especially on clothing. The most popular is the gourd – also one of the essential accoutrements of the Taoist magicians – belonging to Li T'ieh-kuai. He is believed to have been a shaman who returned to the world to inhabit the body of a cripple and is thus normally depicted with a crutch as well. His face is often blue. Another favourite is the fan of Chung-Li Chüan, patron of the military, perhaps because his fan resembles the banners under which the Manchu military were organized.

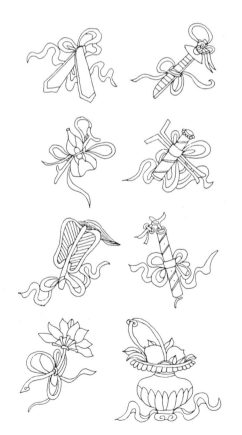

Attributes of the Eight Taoist Immortals.

111

The other Taoist Immortals and their attributes are Lü Dong-bin with sword, He Xian-gu with lotus pod, Lan Xiang-zi with flute, Zhang Guo-Lao with bamboo tube and rods, Cao Guo-jiu with castanets and Lan Cai-he with basket of peaches or flowers.

Chinese language and society

Because of the tonal aspect of Chinese languages two words can be phonetically alike but their meaning distinguished by a different tone of voice. This affords ample opportunity for the symbolic representation of two otherwise unconnected things. Examples in embroidery are legion: 'bat' is the same word, *fu*, phonetically as 'good fortune', and is one of the most common symbols. On exactly the same basis the fish symbolizes abundance and wealth, the carp advantage, the butterfly and chrysanthemum long life, and the vase peace.

Symbols of all kinds permeate Chinese life and thought. Veneration of ancestors, believed to afford access to the next world, and the desire for long life and many sons are expressed by auspicious symbols of longevity and good luck. The dead are believed to enjoy everlasting bliss amidst pine trees with cranes flying above, so that the pine and crane are particularly popular as symbols of long life. Clouds, either banked or as ribbons, provide transport through the heavens for the immortals and thus also symbolize longevity. They can also be interpreted as magic fungus, *lingzhi*.

The attributes of various animals were assigned to the wearer of the embroidery. Mandarin ducks represent connubial bliss. The peacock, a protected bird, is sacred and symbolizes beauty and dignity, as do pheasants and kingfishers. Cocks are honoured as they are believed, as in solar mythology, to drive off the evil spirits of the night. Quails denote bravery. The *ch'i-lin*, a mythical horned animal based on the deer but with dragon-like skin, is a creature of good omen.

The seasons are represented by flowers, and are particularly popular on informal robes. Winter is figured in the Three Friends – the bamboo, pine and plum blossom, spring the iris or magnolia, summer the peony or lotus and autumn the chrysanthemum.

The official court robe, the *ch'i-fu* popularly known as the dragon robe, is a symbol in itself. Its decoration is a magnificent portrayal of the universe. At the hem are wavy lines depicting the cosmic ocean, topped by a bank of mist. At the centre front, back and sides, representing the four cardinal points, rises a triple-peaked mountain, symbolizing the primordial world. Over the rest of the gown, surrounded by clouds and good luck motifs, writhe nine dragons, ancient symbol of imperial power. Eight (the number associated with Taoism and Buddhism) are visible and the ninth, representing man, is hidden on the inner flap. Man inside the robe forms the axis of the universe.

The dragon is an essentially Chinese animal and first appears as a rather snakelike creature on bronze ritual vessels of about 1400 BC. The animals of the hunt of nomadic Central Asia with half-turned head seem later to have been incorporated into this dragon form, as do stags, horses and especially tigers. This writhing dragon, part snake part tiger, originally belonged to an ancient Chinese belief which classified the universe into five elements, each grouped with a colour, animal and cardinal point. The green dragon dwelt in the east, the white tiger in the west, the red bird in the south and the tortoise and snake together comprised the black warrior of the north. They were part of an even older concept, first found depicted on a mirror of the seventh century BC, that divided the cosmos into four directions.

By the Tang era of the seventh century, the dragon and the red bird had become the most auspicious of the animals, featuring on architecture, clothing and decorative arts. The red bird gradually became confused with another mythical bird with exotic tail plumage, the *fenghuang*, also depicted on early ritual bronze vessels of around 1000 BC. This composite bird is commonly referred to as the phoenix, though it is not the same Western legendary phoenix rising from the ashes. Its association with the empress and the female counterbalances the dragon which had come to symbolize imperial power and the male. Both creatures are embroidered on women's and men's clothing.

BUDDHISM

The teaching of Buddha, born in India in about the sixth century BC, is based on the renunciation of desire and the achievement through *nirvana* of a release from the relentless cycle of birth, suffering, death and rebirth. It was disseminated by wandering, begging monks and in the first century AD reached China along the ancient routes whereby silk, ivory, glass and horses were traded between East and West. Here its earliest association with embroidery is to be found.

The region of Central Asia traversed by these trade routes is now mainly desert but was not always so. As mountain glaciers retreated oases dried, burying towns and monasteries under sand, where they lay hidden until the beginning of this century. Tales of cities lost in these desert sands then began to attract the attention of Western archaeologists. Sir Aurel Stein was the first to reach the oasis of Dunhuang in the Gobi desert where thousands of cliff-hewn temples protected the traveller along the ancient silk road. In one of these caves, guarded by an old Buddhist priest, was a small library walled up since the eleventh century. Stein persuaded him to open it and 'in the dim light of the priest's flickering lamp' he discerned piles of rolled-up manuscripts and paintings on silk.

Among the textiles preserved there by the arid climate since the eighth century were a few embroideries. The major work was a large hanging of Buddha preaching, solidly worked in lines of long straight and chain stitch in thick dull floss silk on a hemp cloth lined with silk. The colours are soft shades of beige and orange, with highlights in blue.

A lotus pattern of AD 700–800 decorates the ceiling of a Buddhist cave temple of the Dunhuang oasis in the Gobi desert.

The Buddhist faith of the transit routes to the north of India remained strong in the Tibetan area when Muslims destroyed the monasteries of northern India, and those in Tibet became a repository for Buddhist religious texts. On ceremonial occasions these huge monasteries were covered by enormous embroideries, *thang-ka*, draped over the entire facade, depicting fierce demons or goddesses worked in appliquéd fabric and gilded cardboard, outlined with piping or with yak or horsehair. For ritual dances the lamas wear aprons decorated with the same patterns and techniques.

Depictions of the Buddha himself are one of the subjects of the Burmese embroideries known as *kalagas*, on which he may appear in one of his incarnations. These embroideries decorated temples during festivals or were hung on bullock carts taking people to religious feasts. The work is in appliqué, the figure usually padded and enlivened with ric-rac and sequins.

Actual representations of Buddha were still recently embroidered in Mongolia to decorate the part of the home used for worship. The ritual involved in embroidering a likeness of Buddha required fasting beforehand, washing the hands and burning incense in a quiet room reserved for working. The image of Buddha follows accepted lines but accompanying motifs are freely chosen and drawn with burnt incense sticks.

Buddhism is more often represented in embroidery by its symbols, the most important of which is the lotus. Though pre-eminently Buddhist the lotus is also a potent and complex universal symbol associated with the sun. With its roots in mud, its stem in water and its flower in the air and sun, it symbolizes creative force. As its petals open with sunrise and close with sunset it also represents renaissance and immortality.

With trade goods and people this pattern migrated across Central Asia and was depicted in Buddhist architecture there as an adapted Western acanthus and half-palmette. Lotus patterns, especially of the half-opened flower, are therefore not always instantly recognizable. The petals of the fully opened lotus form a rosette and often resemble a solar symbol.

This fully opened lotus pattern is the central motif on the ceilings of the Buddhist cave temples of Dunhuang. It is also the central motif on cloths used by brides to wrap their dowry, and on marriage canopies from Kathiawar, surrounded by stars and patterns of possible solar origin. On the *kanthas* of Bengal it is almost without exception the central motif. The *kantha* is a quilted cloth, made from old saris and thus incorporating the Buddhist theme of recycling, used to cover beds or wrap precious objects, or for guests to sit on at weddings. The central lotus is often complemented by the tree of life in each corner, several decorative borders and the field filled with symbolic motifs, often solar or Hindu, and with objects from everyday life, such as combs and mirrors.

It is on Chinese embroidery that the symbols of Buddha's enlightenment, known as the Eight Precious Things, are to be found, though

The Eight Buddhist Precious Things.

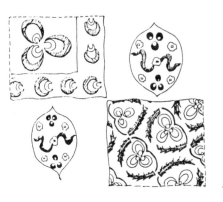

Variations of the Buddhist çintemani *motif on Turkish embroideries of the sixteenth and seventeenth centuries.*

Art and literature of the Uygur Turkish kingdom of Koço in eastern Turkestan (AD 850–1212) and of Dunhuang (AD 911–1016) depict paradise as an assembly of celestial kiosks beside the cosmic Western ocean where fruit trees bear gems and pearls and saints meditate.

considerably less frequently than the attributes of the Eight 1, Immortals. The lotus, the endless knot and the sacred vase are the m, popular.

The vase is again one of the Hundred Antiques, which include books, brushes and other calligraphic materials and also comprise the Eight Secular Precious Things. These also relate largely to scholarly purposes and some are specifically Confucian. Most common on embroidery are the tripod, the two-cash (copper coins with a square hole in the middle), pairs of books, lozenges and horn cups, and a jewel or pearl.

Some confusion exists in the Buddhist symbolism of Chinese embroidery. Buddha's disciples, the Lohans, sometimes appear as the Taoist holy men, and Buddha's dogs, the dogs of Fo, were originally lions. The lion, symbol of power and guardian of sacred buildings in the Middle East, was brought to China from the West, having been used with the same symbolism by the Mughal ruler Ashoka in the third century BC, when he converted to Buddhism and promoted its dissemination eastward. Guardian lions were then depicted at the foot of figures of Buddha, as on the eighth-century embroidery found at Dunhuang. They then gradually evolved into cuddly dogs with frilly ruffs in place of manes. They are often portrayed as a pair chasing each other around a flaming pearl.

The motif of the flaming pearl or jewel sits often at the tip of the dragon's tongue, symbol of imperial treasure. The pearl also symbolizes the Buddhist jewels, of which there are three: Buddha himself, his teaching (*dharma*) and the order of monks and nuns who continued his work (*sangha*).

Three such jewels, with trailing lines or ribbons that were originally bands of clouds, became an important decorative motif adopted by Timur, the fourteenth-century Turkic ruler of a vast Asian empire governed from Samarkand. Depicted as three balls and known as *çintemani* (Buddha's eyes) this pattern came with the Turkic peoples to Turkey where it was a frequent device on Ottoman decorative arts from the sixteenth century. In textiles and embroidery it seems to be connected mainly with the imperial court. Contemporary paintings show sultans wearing gowns with this motif, while their officers and courtiers wear more complex patterning. It came to be known as 'leopard spots' and 'tiger stripes', and denoted power. Each ball capped by a smaller ball inside creates a crescent, a suitable device for the Islamic peoples of Turkey.

A popular motif on Turkish domestic embroideries is a small building and tree known as the 'mosque and cypress'. The absence of a minaret and the juxtaposition of trees indicate that this is not a mosque but the Buddhist cosmological device of a celestial kiosk, *harmĭka*, set in a park by water. The kiosk captures the five directions, that is the four cardinal points leading to the four cosmic oceans and the canopied centre which is Buddha himself under the cupola of heaven. Eighth- and ninth-century paintings of the Uygur Turks of Central Asia show a mountain rising from

The Buddhist kiosk with trees and water and the domed tent as the secular seat of power were popular motifs on nineteenth-century Turkish napkins and towels.

the cosmic ocean topped by this celestial cupola under which the saints meditate. Uygur art and literature represent paradise as a group of such kiosks set in a garden where saints contemplate beside the cosmic western ocean.

The religious significance of the kiosk was lost in the Islamization of Turkey but remained as an architectural concept. The Ottomans, instead of emulating Byzantine architecture, built kiosks in parks by water, as the Topkapi palace complex and the buildings along the Bosphorus which became popular in the nineteenth century as embroidery motifs.

The secular significance of the cupola as the centre of power remained in the domed tents that were an essential part of Ottoman rule. The Seljuks, first of the Turkic tribes to enter Anatolia and who laid the foundations for the later Ottoman civilization, originated as armed nomadic shepherds living in round felt tents known as *yurts*. The Ottomans continued to live in tents and even after the establishment of Bursa as their capital the sultans spent part of each year on the move; and when the prince moved his tent, because of its symbolism, his seat of power moved with him. Turkish miniatures show the sultans in embroidered tents receiving gifts, or on military campaigns in luxuriously decorated encampments. Their sumptuously embroidered tents amazed Western Europeans when Vizir Kara Ustapha was obliged to abandon his on his retreat from Vienna in 1683. The domed tent with trees survives as another important motif of Turkish embroidery.

HINDUISM

The small wayside shrines and intimate domestic altars of India, strewn with offerings of marigolds, glass bangles and misshapen stones, mark the daily immediacy of the panoply of Hindu gods in the local people's lives. The Hindu religion grew from the world of gods and animal deities of the Dravidian Indus valley civilization, absorbing some of the mythology of these early peoples – Indra the sky god, Surya the sun god, Agni the fire god. The Dravidian society was overrun in about 1500 BC by invading Aryans, speaking the Indo-European language of Sanskrit and originating probably from southern Russia. Like all Indo-European groups they were divided into a social hierarchy of three: the priests (*brahmins*), the warriors and the artisans. To these the conquered peoples were added as a fourth group and later a fifth group of tribal poor were denoted as 'untouchables'. From these beginnings developed the Hindu caste system still tenaciously fundamental to Indian society.

Hinduism then developed from the sacred Vedic hymns, from innovations of the brahmins, from the concept of rebirth which gained favour in about 500 BC, from the idea of the all-pervading, universal spirit of god manifest in every living thing, and also from the epic tales of the *Mahabharata* of about 300 BC. These epics recount the legends of hundreds of gods, of whom Vishnu the benevolent (incarnated in Krishna the lover),

Siva the malevolent and the goddess in various forms are the principal trio. The goddess always derives from the primitive mother but can take the form of Vishnu's partner Lakshmi, Siva's consort Parvati, Krishna's lover Radha, or the destructive goddess Kali.

In embroidery it is the legend of Krishna that features most widely on articles that are narrative. Krishna's face is often blue, a holy aspect of Dravidian origin. In his life as a young cowherd Krishna danced with a group of cowgirls (*gopis*) using his divine power to make each believe she was dancing alone with him. The seals of the Indus valley civilization also depict goddesses in a dancing pose from which the *gopis* may derive. On clothing Krishna and his dancing *gopis* are often abstracted into five interlacing squares representing the dancers holding hands.

Temple hangings, Hindu and Jain, commissioned specifically by patrons for their particular sect, emulate painted ones in their mythological storytelling. Otherwise in the immensely varied range of Indian embroidery only two types are narrative. These are the wall friezes, the *pachhitpati* of the Kathiawar peninsula of Gujarat, and the small ceremonial cloths called *rumals* which were made in Chamba in the Punjab.

The *rumals*, embroidered through the eighteenth and nineteenth centuries by the ladies of the court, depict scenes from Hindu epics, probably inspired from the palace wall-paintings, especially from the legends relating to Krishna. They were used to cover gifts to the deities or at weddings and are usually squares of fine bleached cotton, embroidered in muted colours in double darning.

Kathiawar homes comprised two rooms, one for living and the other for storing and displaying textiles. For this room friezes recounting stories of the gods, especially those relating to Krishna as legendary ruler of a Kathiawar kingdom, were embroidered by the women to line the top beam of the wall. Episodes from his life mingle with images of the sun god, of the countryside, animals and other Hindu gods. When made by Kathi women the embroidery is usually in herringbone stitch on cotton with added mirror discs. Friezes commissioned from the professional Mochi, originally cobblers whose fine embroidery was praised by Marco Polo, are worked in chain stitch using a hook known as an ari.

The domestic embroideries of Gujarat are made almost entirely for the dowry, and the women delight especially in picturing those gods that promise fertility and happiness: Krishna still, but also Ganesh the elephant-headed son of Siva. Ganesh is worshipped before any important undertaking, especially marriage, so is frequently embroidered at the centre of the *toran*, the hanging stretched across the top of a doorway as a sign of welcome. Small embroidered or beadworked shrines to Ganesh are also hung in the house on special occasions. The god is stylized to a hardly recognizable form and is flanked by his consorts Siddhi and Buddhi. These hangings are five-sided in shape to recall the actual shrines dedicated to Ganesh.

Other Hindu motifs that are used are the attributes of the gods: the trident of Siva, and the peacock – vehicle of Sarasvati, goddess of wisdom, music and the arts, and a symbol of happiness, love and fertility. The animals of the ancient Indus culture have been retained in Hindu iconography: Ganesh rides on or is accompanied by a rat, Siva's attribute is a bull. Animals as a source of holy power and as a cleanser of the soul are exemplified by the sacred cow, that gentle creature that holds up the Indian traffic while it munches its way through roadside market stall displays.

The *Mahabharata* recounts the legend of the gods churning the milky cosmic ocean, an image which finds its everyday counterpart in the women's regular chore of churning curd. This is a motif often embroidered on the decorative edge of the Kanebi *sadlo*.

Perhaps the greatest influence of Hinduism on embroidery is the caste system. People were forbidden to marry or eat with those outside the *jati*, or subdivision, of their caste and were obliged to follow the trade of their forbears, customs that still have a tenacious hold. Skills and patterns are therefore transferred through generations over hundreds of years and the distinctive styles of domestic embroidery thus vary from caste to caste rather than from village to village.

ISLAM

Islam is the newest of the world's great religions and within a century of Muhammad's migration its proselytizing had established it with amazing rapidity northward into Palestine, Syria, Iran, Iraq and Central Asia and westward through North Africa to Spain and Portugal, and eventually to France where Muslim forces were defeated at Poitiers in AD 732. Subsequent conquests assured it a symbolic crescent of power in the world from South-East Asia to West Africa. Throughout this vast area there is a certain uniformity in artistic and architectural style. Calligraphy, geometry, interlacing, the arabesque, all that subjugates free-flowing art into a disciplined surface-covering decoration are the hallmarks of the Islamic decorative arts. Though the Koran itself does not actually forbid representation of human and animal forms, usage generally does.

Embroidery of the Islamic world has little in the way of style or motifs that come specifically from the Islamic religion, though the deliberate touch of the wrong colour, an unfinished pattern, a fault of stitch encapsulate the belief that only Allah is perfect.

The earliest example of Islamic calligraphy in embroidery is the work known as *tiraz*, decorative bands inserted at the armhole seam of the robes of rulers and persons of note throughout most of the Islamic world. Woven or embroidered, they were made in workshops in Egypt and at Sana'a in Yemen during the Abbasid dynasty of Baghdad (AD 749–1258) and the Fatamid of Egypt, North Africa and Syria (AD 909–1170). Inscriptions are embroidered in red, black or silver thread and comprise the name of the

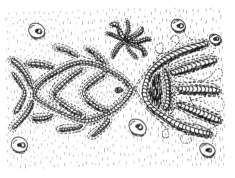

The fish and hand of Fatima are Islamic amulets against the evil eye and are ubiquitous motifs in Tunisian embroidery and jewelry.

caliph, a religious invocation, the name of the weaving workshop and the date. In the later Fatamid period such comprehensive information yielded to large geometric pattern, plant and animal motifs and the expression of some simple pious hope.

Intricate Islamic patterning in embroidery is best exemplified by the Hispano-Mauresque embroideries of Spain which were made, probably in the provinces of Granada and Toledo, while the Arabs were still in possession of much of the Iberian peninsula. These handmade linen cloths are almost or entirely covered with floss silk stitchery in salmon, yellow, brown, red and shades of blue. The strict geometric patterning, which closely resembles Islamic tiles, was marked out by professional artists. The embroiderer then outlined the design with linen thread in stem stitch and filled the spaces with long-armed cross stitch. This stitch was probably introduced to the Iberian peninsula by the Moors.

Embroideries with a specifically Islamic purpose include the small cloths made by the Shi'ite Hazara of Afghanistan to wrap their *mohr* (prayer stones). These are of terracotta and should come from Karbela, a place of pilgrimage. The *mohr* is kept wrapped in the cloth which for prayer is laid on a prayer mat. The design – worked most commonly in long satin stitch in multicoloured silk and either of radiating geometric pattern or pictorial with mosques, minarets and hands – indicates where the *mohr* should be placed so that the forehead of the prostrate worshipper touches it. The cloth is considered a holy object and should never be sold or used for any other purpose. It must also never be used in a household where there are menstruating or pregnant women.

In north-western India, in the isolated region of Kutch along the border with Pakistan where Muslim and Hindu live side by side, many traditions, even as basic to Hinduism as caste or to Islam as purdah, are shared. Dress styles can also be interchanged, but in general the Muslim women distinguish themselves by the cut of their dress and particularly by the fineness of their embroidery. The Dhanetah women may take anything up to three years to work the front bodice panel on their *churi*, the long dress that is the most important item of their dowry. If the woman has herself made the pilgrimage to Mecca, she will not include mirrorwork in this embroidery.

The fish as protective device – like hands, horns, the cross and the solar rosette – frequently decorates the threshold of a house.

Here and across the Pakistani border in Sind Islamic women embroider masks for their wedding and small bags to hold the Koran; in Bangladesh it is wrapping cloths that fulfil this purpose. The Koran, the teaching and laws of God divulged to Muhammad in Arabic, plays a supreme role in the Islamic world. More than just a book it is God incarnate. Excerpts from it are deemed to have the power to ward off evil and are often encased in silver jewelry. They can also be inserted into amulets appliquéd on to costume.

The talismanic role of pattern is of immense importance in the Islamic world where motifs such as the fish, and the hand of Fatima (*khomsa*), as well as amulets of crescents, triangles and squares are believed to deflect evil spirits. Painted hands and fish protect houses from India to Egypt and embroidered versions dominate the costume of Tunisia.

ZOROASTRIANISM

Zoroastrianism is a Persian religion established by Zarathustra, a figure of whom little is known for sure but who is accepted as having lived in eastern Iran around the seventh/sixth century BC. The religion he founded was monotheistic with theological concepts of good and evil, spirit and flesh, light and dark, heaven and hell, which strongly influenced other world faiths. In its later phases it accepted minor deities including Mithra the sun god. It is probably best known for its fire temples, its practice of hanging the dead on Towers of Silence to be picked apart by vultures and most of all for its priests, the Magi, to whom the three wise men who came from the East bringing gifts to the infant Jesus belonged.

Under the Sassanid dynasty (AD 226–650) Zoroastrianism spread westward to the Persian gulf and eastward to Afghanistan and the Indus valley. From about the eighth century on, after persecution by the Muslims, some Zoroastrians settled on the west coast of India where they are known as Parsees, a corruption of Persians.

Zoroastrians in Iran form a minority group settled in the province of Kerman and around Yezd on the edge of the great salt desert. The women wear a distinctive shift of counterbalanced red and green silk embroidered with countless little animals, fish and plants in heavy multicoloured twist silk. The same animals are worked on the baggy trousers made of brightly coloured strips of fabric with tie-dye circles. With these is worn a red tie-dye shawl or, for marriage, a black or dark indigo silk one with the same animals and a large sun motif or circle of animals in the centre. A peacock often features on the shawl, closely resembling those on the satin skirts of Gujarat, where many Parsees settled. The Zoroastrians also wore white garments worked with small cross stitch motifs of animals and trees.

CHRISTIANITY
Biblical narrative

The decorative arts of the early Middle Ages in Western Europe were a hymn to the glory of God, recounting and praising the lives of Christ and the saints. Most of the embroidery surviving from this period is also ecclesiastical, a tradition which through a series of lapses and revivals such as the Reformation and Counter Reformation, is still thriving today. In secular embroidery the contribution of the Christian church is particularly evident in the sixteenth and seventeenth centuries. Linen cloths and canvaswork furnishings were in the same narrative style as other decorative arts: just as stained glass windows instructed the illiterate, so did embroidery.

continued on page 129

RELIGION AND ITS PATTERNS

TAOISM

15 Hanging, Hong Kong. The attributes of the Eight Taoist Immortals are among the most popular of all Chinese motifs. On this hanging are Lü Dong-bin with sword and Chang Guo-Lao with bamboo tube and rods.

16 Hanging, China. The Chinese believed in many gods: of wealth, longevity and of the kitchen – a family deity who apportioned the length of days, wealth of the household and noted the inhabitants' vices and virtues. Another was Kuan Ti, god of war.

17 Child's bodice, China. Symbolism permeates Chinese life: the dead are believed to enjoy everlasting bliss amidst pine trees and cranes, so that both denote longevity.

118 Dragon robe, ch'i-fu, China. The official Chinese court robe, it is a symbol in itself. Nine dragons, ancient symbol of imperial power, are accompanied by the Taoist gourd and basket of peaches, the crane and the flaming pearl.

119 Woman's jacket, China. The phoenix is associated with the empress and is often worked on women's clothes. The Taoist attributes are woven into the damask fabric.

BUDDHISM

120 Below: Cloth, Mongolia. Buddha decorates cloths for the house altar.

121 Ashon, Bengal. The lotus is the central motif of kanthas. This ashon shows the Hindu goddess Lakshmi and the rath.

122 Sleeve cuff of robe, China. The sacred vase is a Buddhist symbol and is also one of the Chinese Hundred Antiques. The bat symbolizes happiness.

123 Towel, Turkey. The Buddhist cosmological device of a celestial kiosk harmîka set in a park by water was a theme of the arts of the Uygur Turks of Central Asia and is frequent in Turkish embroidery.

HINDUISM

124   Door hanging, toran, Gujarat, India. Ganesh, the elephant-headed son of Siva, promises fertility and happiness and is worshipped before any important undertaking. His image is therefore often the central motif of the cloths hung across the door at festivities.

125   Temple hanging, pichhavai, Mochi caste, Gujarat, India. The Hindu legend of Krishna dancing with the cowgirls, gopis, is one of the most popular embroidery themes.

ISLAM

126   Woman's skirt, Aleppo, Syria. Though the Koran does not expressly forbid the portrayal of human forms usage generally does and anthropomorphic motifs are rare in Islamic embroidery. The figure is combined with the fertility symbol of the carnation, which in the embroidery of northern Syria is stylized into a hexagon.

127 *Fragment, Hispano-Mauresque, Spain. Intricate Islamic patterning in embroidery is best exemplified by the Hispano-Mauresque cloths of Spain made while the Arabs were still in possession of the peninsula. The designs closely resemble those of Islamic tiles and were marked out by professional artists.*

128 *Prayer cloth, Hazara, Afghanistan. The Shi'ite Hazara embroider small mats to wrap their prayer stones. The cloths were considered holy objects and should never be sold or used in a household where there are menstruating or pregnant women.*

ZOROASTRIANISM

129 *Marriage shawl, Persia. Zoroastrian embroidery is distinctive with its small animals worked in thick twist silk both on the dresses of the women, which are of counterbalanced red and green silk, and on their dark indigo silk marriage shawls.*

CHRISTIANITY

130 Casket, England. Biblical stories were the theme of English stumpwork of the seventeenth century, on pictures, caskets and mirror frames. The tale of David and Bathsheba was a favourite: here David is seated under a canopy while Bathsheba bathes in a pool.

131 Hanging, Portugal. The pelican in her piety, symbol of Christ's sacrifice, is one of the designs in Vinciolo's pattern book published in Venice in 1587. It became, with the Agnus Dei and Adam and Eve, a popular Christian motif in secular embroidery.

132 *Alms bag, Italy. In Catholic countries the holy monograms of IHS and IMR or M occur frequently in secular embroidery. In particular IMR with a motif of Madonna and child is a design of Belgian samplers. The holy monograms were believed to hold power over evil and were also often carved above doorways.*

133 *Sampler, Nürnberg, Germany (1728). The instruments of Christ's passion feature on many continental samplers, propagated by pattern books such as Jean le Clerc's 1613 reprint of Vinciolo. The form of Nürnberg samplers of the seventeenth and early eighteenth century was always a central two-handled vase of flowers with upholstery patterns and scattered motifs mainly from Sibmacher's pattern book of 1597, such as the seated stag and the peacock.*

Sources of biblical designs were the pattern books first printed in Germany in the early sixteenth century. The Bible woodcuts published by Bernard Saloman and Jean de la Tournes in Lyon in 1553 were copied all over Europe, while in England it was those of Gerard de Jode published in Antwerp in 1585 that proved most popular. As woodcuts and engravings of classical mythology and allegories were copied equally assiduously it seems evident that by the time these themes came into the hands of the amateur needlewoman they were chosen merely for their decorative qualities, rather than from deep-rooted religious faith.

A blend of tableaux from the Old Testament, Greek and Roman mythology and hunting scenes worked in wild yellow silk in chain or back stitch, feature on quilts made mainly around Hughli in Bengal in the time of Portuguese patronage from the late sixteenth century to the collapse of their power in India in 1632.

Individual motifs

Individual motifs of Christian origin, as opposed to biblical narrative, are found in secular embroidery, particularly in white household linen and in lacis or filet work, and were also disseminated by pattern books. The pelican in her piety, symbol of Christ's sacrifice, is one of the designs in Vinciolo's pattern book published in Venice in 1587. From Sibmacher comes the Agnus Dei in his *Schön Neues Modelbuch* published in Nürnberg in 1597, and St Michael and the dragon, Christian image of the folkloric victory of good over evil, in his *Neues Modelbuch in Kupffer gemacht* of 1601. In Catholic countries the holy monograms of IHS and M were believed to hold power over evil and were also frequently chosen.

As floral designs came to dominate European embroidery from the mid-seventeenth century, so the Christian motifs survived in children's samplers, especially those of continental Europe. A great range of biblical motifs occur: the crucifix with the instruments of the passion and the sun and moon, recalling Luke's description of the darkening of the sky at Christ's death, Adam and Eve, Jacob fighting the angel, the spies from Canaan. Some of these survive as occasional motifs on such linen items as display towels, particularly Adam and Eve.

The cross

The cross is a universal symbol of such antiquity that it cannot always be ascribed to a purely Christian source, but in certain instances one can be quite sure of its origin: in the case of the embroidered cross on a child's knitted sock of the Coptic Christians of Egypt, and the staggered cross motif of Rumanian shirt sleeves that is also the design stamped on consecrated bread for the Orthodox church, for example. There are also two outstanding examples of a cross used on costume as a declaration of affiliation to the Christian church in the midst of a society of Islamic faith. These are found on the festive shawls of the women of Qaracoche in Iraq and the shifts of the women of the villages around the mountain town of Livno in Bosnia, Yugoslavia.

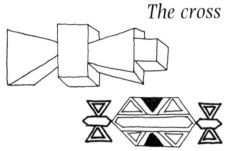

The seal in the form of a staggered cross, used to stamp consecrated bread, serves as an embroidery motif on Rumanian blouse sleeves.

The festive shawl of the women of Qaracoche is embroidered in bright rough stitchery with motifs declaring their Christian faith in a Muslim society: the cross in particular but also scenes of an Orthodox altar with priests officiating.

Qaracoche is a Christian village of around 6,000 people in a region of northern Iraq where most communities are of mixed faith. Over their caftan the women wear a draped shawl tied on the shoulder, of which the festive version – *châl* – is richly, if crudely, embroidered. A cross always forms the centre motif and further crosses are scattered around, for a large number is thought to bring luck. Here and there is a scene depicting priests officiating at an altar, a ritual fascinating to the women who, though Christian, are seated a long way from the altar as they are thought to be unclean. Other motifs include a flower enclosed in a serrated leaf, very reminiscent of the Turkish *saz* motif, and a crescent moon shape, both believed to offer magic protection and avert evil spirits. Birds and dancing women fill the rest of the shawl. The embroidery is in bright floss silks on black or check wool of red and black, and is worked with stem stitch outlines filled with rough satin stitch. It is done by women specialized in the task, with the client choosing the designs from the traditional repertoire. The woman is buried in her *châl*.

Half a dozen villages around Livno in western Yugoslavia have retained their Orthodox faith in a region that is strongly Islamic. The women of these villages are distinguished by their shifts known as 'cross shifts'. Made of homegrown handspun linen embroidered in red and blue goatshair they have a large red cotton cross appliquéd on each sleeve. The shift was worn for the first time for the wedding ceremony, together with the large white cotton headscarf similarly appliquéd with red cotton which the woman had been allowed to wear as a young girl as soon as she was considered marriageable. A heavy sleeveless woollen jacket and tapestry-woven apron, with motifs that varied according to the woman's age, completed the outfit. After the wedding the shift would be kept for festive occasions during the first year of the woman's married life or until her first child was born, after which it was carefully folded away to be handed on to her daughter.

4

THE MAGICAL SOURCE
OF PROTECTION

EVIL SPIRITS

The modern Japanese businessman travels with ticket and insurance; the Yugoslav requiring medical treatment has doctors, drugs and hospitals at his disposal. In the early years of this century both relied on magic for their well-being, which involved, for the sick man, having a black cat slit open, laid across his stomach and left to rot; for the traveller, carrying on his person an inscription bearing the character *tsuchi*, 'earth', preferably written in vermilion ink as red was thought to be particularly distasteful to spirits.

The traveller left his home, which was known to be protected by guardian spirits, to set forth along roads that were infested with evil beings and haunted by wandering souls. Animals lay in wait ready to transform themselves into spirits to do him harm, demons tarried at crossroads and beside muddy tracks. To confront these dangers he used, as embroideries do, both pattern and material. Earth from his home was essential for his survival in strange regions even in the form of a written character, for characters were considered not only to represent the object, as a word or pattern does, but also to hold the spirit of that object: the character was as potent as the earth itself.

It is sometimes hard for us to realize that within living memory people inhabited – and indeed some still do — a world they believed controlled by supernatural beings both good and evil. Every spinney, every copse, every crossroads, every stream, every stone held its own spirit; every culture had its own hobgoblins. In Islamic belief there were not only men and angels but also a third class of beings made of fire, *jinns*. The Indians believed in witches and liver-eaters – *jiggerkhars* – who just by looking at a person could steal their liver and kill them.

Magical powers were not confined to supernatural beings, but were held also by women. Human conception was not understood and when in the eighteenth century it was first established that it was the result of sexual intercourse the claim was greeted with derision. Women's ability to

The patterns decorating houses with the purpose of protecting their inhabitants from evil are also used on clothing.

produce children was therefore regarded as miraculous and their fertility was protected by decoration.

Women could also be feared and reviled as witches. Among the Ghiliak and Néghidales, peoples who live around the basin of the Amour river in eastern Siberia, embroiderers are the worst witches of all. In the loops made by their threads they can ensnare the souls of people in their presence. The Ghiliak verb *tcagcott* has two meanings: to embroider patterns and to cast spells. Men do not embroider nor would they approach a woman doing so for fear that watching the threads being twisted around would cause them to become disorientated when hunting.

Women could also house the evil eye – the most feared of all spirits, for the eye is the mirror of the soul. In the Siwa oasis of the western desert of Egypt widows were believed to possess the evil eye and were clothed in white and imprisoned for four months until considered clean. In the late 1980s Reuter reported that a synagogue in Israel had stopped admitting women because of a series of disasters in the area for which it was believed women with their evil eye were responsible.

The evil eye is envious and wishes to destroy perfection: brides and babies are particularly vulnerable. It, and evil spirits in general, can attack the body and cause illness or even death. Against them three aspects of embroidered decoration are considered effective – the position in which the embroidery is placed, patterns that hold a mystic power, and assertive materials. The evil eye especially can be overpowered by anything that dazzles and makes it blink, such as shiny objects, pieces of metal, coins, buttons, mirror that reflects and holds its image; by anything that tinkles and distracts it; by objects that can pierce it, particularly triangular ones holding the power of the trinity and the feminine mystique; by gaudy bright colours; by alternating colours along edges; and by anything that confuses it through asymmetrical pattern where it loses its way.

The evil eye and *jinns* are still greatly feared in the Islamic world and there the protective devices of embroidery are usually consciously employed. Often, however, the choice of pieces of mirror, alternating colours and the like have become almost subconscious, as has superstition in the West. A black cat brings good luck in some Western countries, bad luck in others and is still in our children's books the associate of every witch though we never pause to wonder why. Viruses attack our computers on Friday the 13th, we cross our fingers walking under ladders, perform pagan topping-out ceremonies on our new airport buildings, and decorate our Easter buns with a cross to keep away evil spirits that might prevent the dough from rising – a protective pattern also found in embroidery worldwide.

Positioning

Costume in general and embroidery in particular play a protective role both physical and spiritual. Those evil spirits likely to attack the body are kept out by decorative devices at every edge and opening. From Asia to

Western Europe embroidery is commonly placed encircling the neck, along hem and cuff, around pockets and also at buttonholes. Seams are closed with decorative stitchery and certain vulnerable places carry heavy embroidery. These are the front bodice, the shoulders and sleeves and often also the sexual area and the centre back. Even when they cover much of the garment these areas of embroidery never intermingle but are always clearly defined. In each case such embroidery was destined to protect these specific and significant parts of the body. Most heavily embroidered – and the last item of Western European costume to disappear – was the coif: as can be seen in any village of Eastern Europe the headscarf and apron still linger as everyday wear, though they serve no practical purpose.

Edgings and seams
Strengthening It must not be forgotten that while decorative stitchery on edges and seams is believed to afford magical protection it also physically strengthens. In man's earliest clothing a decorative effect must already have been achieved by stitching skins together with sinew. Such thonging leaves gaps which could then be filled with ornament. A similar opportunity for embellishment can occur with appliqué, where a piece of fabric may first be applied to cover a hole, then repeated to make a pattern and then suggested by outline stitchery alone, as on the patched raffia cloths of the Kuba of Zaire. On the sheepskin coats of Hungary such patches are known as 'witch patches'.

The strengthening action of stitchery is apparent in the vocabulary used to describe Palestinian costume, where edgings are of extreme importance, the back hem being the most significant. Zigzag appliqués are known as *tishrifeh*, meaning 'to make good', and form a row of triangles considered a protective amulet, a *hejab*. Bands of fishbone stitch in striped colours, when edging necks and cuffs, are called *habkeh*, 'to make stronger'. On village dresses hems are finished with a band of appliquéd fabric on the inside and decorative stitching on the outside. On Bedouin dresses hems are deeper, with several rows of satin stitch, giving the strong finish needed for walking in the desert.

The strengthening role of embroidery is also apparent in other desert clothes – trouser cuffs are thickly stitched, those of Yemen to afford protection against thorns, and those of the Qutayfé area of Syria against prickly straw and thistles.
Neck The edging to which the main attention is directed varies with different countries. In most it is the neck that bears the finest work: Baluchi dresses have rows of exquisitely fine stitchery; the Tcheremiss of Siberia border the necks of their dresses with shells, with the specific purpose of protecting from the evil eye; in Norway the coloured edging at the neck identified the district the wearer came from.

Though in most countries it is usually the front of the neck opening that is especially highly decorated, sometimes the nape is of greater signifi-

The insertion of a dazzling piece of appliqué inside the hem of a garment became a device of costume in much of the Ottoman empire. An early example is on a kaftan belonging to the Turkish sultan Şehzade Korkut (1470–1513).

cance. The wedding dresses of Thano Bula Khan in Pakistan have a neck slit flanked by small pockets of sand from the girl's home village, permeated with strong-smelling spices to protect her in her new surroundings, in the same way as his home earth protected the Japanese traveller. The dress is worn for marriage with these pockets at the nape, after which it is turned and worn with the slit to the front. Frequently decoration of the nape was not in fact on the dress itself but on a hanging headdress. An old marriage coif of Madhia in Tunisia bears as its only ornamentation an inscription at the nape of the neck worked in flat silver thread which has tarnished with time but on which 'that protection may last' is still just legible, expressing a hope of some magical safeguard.

Hem In Turkey, in Syria and in many parts of the Ottoman empire, and also as far west as Moravia, an intricate and colourful piece of appliquéd fabric in a complex or jagged shape is worked inside the hem at the openings of a garment. In Syria the fabric is usually silk ikat and the outline of its shape is stitched in red on the outside of the garment; in Moravia the appliqué is in red wool. With movement a dazzling effect is achieved. Similar patterns are occasionally hidden inside sleeves, as with the sheepskin coats of Hungary.

Seams The most frequent decoration for seams is colour alternation, commonly of a stitch that straddles the two pieces of fabric, such as fishbone, buttonholing or faggoting. This device is to be found from Asia through the Middle East to Eastern Europe. Red is frequently alternated with white or with green, and colours can be paired or in multiples. Even where the women are predominately weavers and their clothes carry almost no embroidery, as in Jordan or Djerba, the seams joining the handwoven loom widths will be accentuated with striped stitchery.

In the Türkmen embroidery of Central Asia and in Eastern Europe, the selvedge of the fabric when coloured is left visible as a supplementary decoration to the seam embroidery. The shifts of the Dinaric mountains of Yugoslavia, for example, though always embroidered in copper, blue and green, will have visible red selvedges at the seams.

In Rumania the word for ornamental stitchery on seams is *cheite*, meaning 'little key', the word also used for the house and courtyard key. Keys, invented by the bronzesmith Theodore of Samos in the sixth century BC, always had quasi-magical powers. Travellers in medieval France, for instance, branded them on their horse or donkey for safety on the road.

Breasts

Though seldom as blatantly as in the 'Viking breastplate' style of the embroidered blouses of Kutch, women's breasts – as the source of life for the newborn baby – are frequently covered by heavy embroidery. In Europe they were protected by the detached stomacher, ornate with stitchery: in gold on those of peasant France, for instance, and with an unchanging tree of life motif on those of Pilsen in Bohemia.

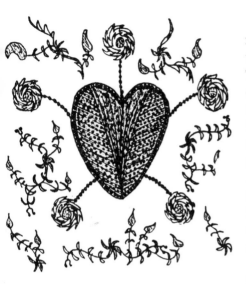

The stomachers of Pilsen are always embroidered with a version of the tree of life as a heart.

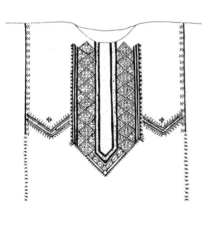

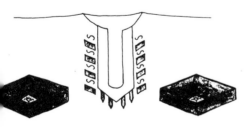

The shifts of the Tcheremiss and Tchuvash women of Siberia protect the breasts with symbolic embroidery.

Heavy metal breast clasps were typical of the Finno-Ugric peoples and much of the most emphatic decoration over breasts is to be found among their descendants living in central Russia and western Siberia. The Tcheremiss of the Kazan region on the Volga river east of Moscow embroider the front of their rough hemp shifts with a V-shaped pattern they call 'guardian of the breasts'. The Tchuvash, descendants of the Volga Bulgars who live in the same region, appliqué red fabric in a diamond shape over the breasts, leaving a gap over the nipple. Here they embroider a small, plant-derived motif in blue and beige silk, or sometimes in red. Alternatively they embroider a solid geometric motif with an 8-pointed star at its centre and hooked motifs at the edges, in red with touches of beige and green. The neck edges and underarm gussets of these shifts are commonly of blue, blue/red or blue/white fabric and red cotton is appliquéd along most other edges and seams.

The women of the Evank-Tungus, hunters of the forests of eastern Siberia who are highly tattooed, have embroidery on the breast area of their shifts that shows their origin and clan. The Mordvinians, a larger group who live in the Volga region, wear breast ornaments of leather embroidered with red cloth, shells, glass beads and brass ornaments.

In Bahriyah, one of the oases of the western desert of Egypt – now linked to Cairo by road where previously it was nine to ten days' camel ride away – the women's traditional dress is a wide black cotton shift with breasts and pockets accentuated by contrasting colour and stitch. The linear embroidery over the front of the dress is in raspberry-red floss silk in double herringbone – with the shoulders and top sleeve surface further emphasized with extra stitching or metal discs – while the embroidery over the breasts and pockets is sharply divergent with its green and orange cross stitch.

Sexual area

The purpose of the ubiquitous apron of most European peasant costume, and particularly that of Eastern Europe, is symbolically protective and not practical. Varying in style with each village but normally heavily embroidered, intricately pleated or finely woven in striped patterning, it covered a dress or petticoat that almost always was deliberately left plain where the apron would be worn. It is the antithesis of an apron worn to protect precious clothing. Instead it protects the body.

The ritual associations of the apron are many. In Transylvania it was worn inside-out for mourning; in Hungary it formed part of the costume of unmarried men and the bridegroom; an illegitimate child in Rumania was said to be 'from the apron'; but mainly it was everywhere associated with marriage. This was the moment at which the bride, as well as taking a new hairstyle and headdress, changed the type of apron she had worn as a young girl to another that declared her status as a married woman. Sometimes, as in Rumania, the materials used to decorate it were a gift

A feature of the costume of the newly-wed Erza Mordvinian bride of the Volga region was the back apron, common also in Eastern European dress. The wimple hat was worn by the bride only for a short while after the wedding. It went out of fashion about the time of the First World War.

from the bridegroom and the apron, often of red fabric, would be used in the marriage ritual or carried through the streets in the wedding procession, hung from a pole like a flag for all to see. Women of the nomadic Sarakatsani, now living mainly in Greece, embroidered twenty to forty aprons (*panoules*) during their youth, each with different symbolism – such as the cross, the serpent, or the moon – that showed the woman's social status or was thought suitable for various occasions and moods. She would then choose each day the appropriate one to wear. The apron – the *podia* – of all Greek costume was imbued with magical properties – in Thrace, for example, it is thrown over the stomach of a woman in labour to facilitate the birth.

Throughout Europe styles of apron differed not only from village to village or with the marital status of the woman, but also with everyday or festive wear. Festive ones were obviously more ornate. For everyday use, the upper half of the two-part apron of Russia, for example, was embroidered and the bottom fringed, while the festive version has brass chains, beads and shells added to the embroidery. In Blata in Bohemia festive aprons were covered in beadwork and sequins, negating any possible practical role, while those of Croatia and Bosnia were covered in coins and edged with red triangles. They were often hung from the neck. Almost everywhere the usual edgings of bobbin lace, crochet or embroidery were deeper, and insertions – such as the central vertical bands of bobbin lace, needleweaving, embroidery in alternating colours or floral ribbons of the aprons of Czechoslovakia – were more decorative. When embroidered, both everyday and festive aprons featured mainly flower designs or symbols of fertility such as the pomegranate.

In many areas of Eastern Europe a back apron was also worn, or the back was often hung with brocaded floral ribbons. Among more primitive peoples it is also often the buttocks that are decorated. An example is the Mru tribe of the Chittagong Hill Tracts in Bangladesh. Their simple skirts made of a band of cloth edged with small beads have a central panel of patterned weaving supplemented by light embroidery.

Dresses which carry embroidery specifically over the sexual region are a feature of the costume of some of the Muslim peoples of north-west India and Pakistan. Women of the Khatrie clan, dyers of Kutch, wear a shift, an *aba*, which is decorated in a deep panel over the chest with a pendant pattern of exceptional fineness worked below the waist. Even when the dress is decorated with couched metal braiding or in the tie-dye technique the same disposition of pattern is adhered to. When embroidered the work is of tiny pieces of mirror with open chain and extremely fine interlacing stitch. A red silk version is worn for marriage and is one of the dowry gifts presented by the groom. The Seyhud farming community wear dresses of the same type.

The silk dresses of the Baluch of Pakistan, in addition to embroidery at the breasts, shoulder and neck, have a deep rectangular pocket called a *pudo* down the centre front of the skirt, embroidered at the top in an upwardly pointed triangle that lies over the pudendum.

Protective embroidery on a dress is often placed slightly higher than the sexual region so that it lies over a pregnant stomach, as on the sunburst decoration on the dresses of the Siwa oasis, where the most densely embroidered squares with buttons lie over the breasts and stomach. In the costume of many countries embroidery edging the neck slit ends in extensive patterning over the stomach.

Belts carry immensely important sexual symbolism but this is more concerned with how or when they are worn than with the embroidery on them. In North Africa on 'the day of the belt' the bride resumes her normal life; in Oltenia, Rumania, a metal belt which must have been made by a naked gypsy in one night, was worn before childbirth to protect the foetus from evil spirits and to relieve childbirth pains. This belt was hung with amulets, which included in particular keys to facilitate the passage of the baby, and axes and knives to encourage the birth of a boy. These amulets were suspended across the apron, which thus carried no embroidery.

The embroidery on a belt occasionally held some meaning: men of Alpine regions, for example, wore wide belts covered in quillwork that was meant to pinpoint the source of their courage and virility. It could also denote a trade: boatmen on the canals of England wore wide canvas belts embroidered in multicoloured wools with spiderweb patterns in squares, made for them by their womenfolk.

The head

Embroidered headgear is breathtaking in its variety: white and gold coifs of Europe, tribal caps of Central Asia, skull caps of the Jewish and Islamic worlds, pixie-hoods of North Africa, coin caps of the Finno-Ugric and Turkic peoples, beaded and feathered headdresses of the North-American Indian, head and face veils of the Middle East covered in talismanic materials such as tassels, shells, buttons and blue beads. In many societies headgear accentuated an unnatural shape, as the head was not only protected by coverings but also deliberately deformed for magical as well as social reasons – the coifs of France serve as one example, where distorting the head by binding was practised until the end of the nineteenth century.

Hair was universally regarded as magical, a concentration of the life force of the person, and was particularly potent in the Judaeo-Christian and American Indian traditions. In the Paracas culture snakes shared the supernatural powers of hair, and burial turbans were decorated with serpentine patterning.

Hair was also, like nails, a part of the body from which pieces could be cut and then, retaining its spiritual strength, fall into the hands of witches. Women's hair especially was believed to possess magical force in its power of seduction. In Russia women were considered impure and only their hair was clean, and girls' tresses were plaited with totem animals in tin. In

The bride's hair is prepared for the marriage headdress, never to be uncovered in public again.

Heavy shoulder ornamentation features on a figurine of 3000 BC from Turkestan and on a Russian stone statue of the eleventh to twelfth century.

almost every society girls' hair was highly decorated and then at marriage covered with great ceremony by a headdress. After this the woman never again uncovered it, even hiding it from her husband and wearing a bonnet in bed. She was especially careful never to show the nape, and scarves or headdresses with embroidered flaps are common wear for married women. Embroidery could be placed on the actual head section or on the extension. Long flaps decorated with stitchery or with materials that flashed or dazzled were common in much of the costume of Europe. The bridal dress of Lindnorst in Germany, for example, has the back of the head entirely hung with ribbons holding mirrors to avert the evil eye.

An extended version of the hanging headcovering was the *chyrpy* of the Tekke Türkmen women, a cloak worn draped over a high headdress, the main motif of which was the fertility symbol of the tulip. The skull caps of their children, ornately embroidered in the same style, were often hung with coins and amulets. Similar caps worn by the men, children and unmarried girls of the Uzbek, another people of Central Asia, clearly had a symbolic meaning, for a new mother would ask another woman who had brought up a healthy child to make her baby's cap for her.

In many places the source of life was believed to lie in the ear and special protection was provided by heavy embroidery or by strategically placed pattern or material. A triangular amulet of fabric or an embroidered cross was positioned over the ear on children's caps. But often – particularly in Europe – it was with embroidery on the shoulder of the linen shift or shirt that the ear was afforded protection from ill.

Shoulders and sleeves

On the linen shifts and shirts of Europe the disposition of embroidery on shoulders and sleeves is specific and relative to the construction of the garment. Its density is often linked to the seam which with a straight cut will fall across the upper arm. Heavy shoulder embroidery follows this seam or lies above it. Decoration in this position features on a Russian figurine of the eleventh to twelfth century.

Significantly, while the traditional *huipil* of Central American costume is normally brocaded with motifs from local iconography, the imported item of the blouse is embroidered following its sleeve construction with European motifs of flowers and animals.

In the distinctive and rigid disposition of the shift sleeves of Bucovina in north-east Rumania the seam area is worked in a band, called an *altita*, of fine pulledwork, brocading or pastel-coloured embroidery, while above it the shoulder is thickly worked. Below the *altita* narrow vertical or diagonal lines of small embroidery motifs continue to the cuff. These are known as *rîuri*, or rivers: the swift rivers which flow through the villages were always believed to have magic powers.

On many linen shifts of Eastern Europe the embroidery extends in a panel from the shoulder over the entire upper arm surface but is always separated from the cuff, which remains an edging decoration. It is easy to recognize the protective power of the arm raised across the body, or even at rest at the sides, and the consequent relevance of this part of costume.

The straight-cut narrow sleeves of most dresses and blouses of north-west India and Pakistan are also embroidered down their whole length ending with a distinct cuff edging. There is frequently a separate and dominant motif on the shoulder that is solar in origin.

Where decorative bands descend from the shoulder to the chest, rather than down the arm, shoulder embroidery can also recall the cut of the shift known as the *tunica manicata* or *tunica dalmatica*, worn at the decline of the Roman empire. Shoulders can also be worked as epaulettes of almost military importance, as in the jackets of Albania and Tunisia.

Sleeves as a separate item in themselves were a ritual object, their importance perhaps deriving, as so much in peasant costume, from the dress of aristocrats and bourgeois of earlier periods. The heavy silk sleeves of medieval upper class costume may find a counterpart in the ballooning sleeves of so many villagers, intricately pleated or embroidered in a distinctly local style. Such sleeves, often of a finer fabric than the rest of the garment, formed part of the dowry for both bride and groom. In Hungary a grandmother would start embroidering sleeves for her granddaughter as soon as the child was born, devoting most of her time to this task until the girl was married. The girl herself made sleeves for her groom, sewing them to a shirt only after the engagement when she was sure of his size.

Embroidery on the sleeves of Chinese costume, unless part of the overall design, is concentrated on the cuff and plays no particular protective role. The cut of clothing stems from earlier clothing of animal skin or of cloth. The sleeve derived from the skin clothing of the nomadic Manchu, designed for riding horses over steppelands, is long and narrow with a horsehoof cuff covering and protecting the hand. On court costume the body of this sleeve is plain or ribbed and pushed back to facilitate arm and hand movements, and the cuff is embroidered with motifs conforming to Chinese symbolism and aesthetics. The sleeve of clothing derived from the cloth tradition is enormously long and wide, designed as a display of wealth in its yards of silk and as a modest cover for hands considered unseemly to display in public. The cuff is embroidered in a straight band in a style unrelated to the patterning on the main body of the garment. The Chinese man, bowing slightly with clasped hands, thus shields the front of his body with a silken muff depicting delicate landscapes of figures, pagodas, bridges and butterflies and those floral tributes to the seasons – peonies, chrysanthemums or narcissus.

Pockets

Pockets are nearly always strengthened and protected by embroidered patterning. The eighteenth-century dandy of most of Europe wore a silk waistcoat or jacket with floral embroidery at the edges and around the

The openings of pockets are frequently almost concealed in a splendour of protective embroidery, as on the shift of a manservant of one of the beys of Tunis.

pockets; the pockets of the Englishwoman of the same period – two pear-shaped bags hung from a tape round her waist – were delicately embroidered, usually with trailing floral designs or with canvaswork, though they were buried unseen beneath her petticoats.

In peasant costume the asymmetrical aspect of protective embroidery is often linked with pockets. They are placed out of alignment or are false, to distract the evil eye. The men's jackets of Brittany, *chupenn*, are embroidered round the pockets with zigzags, strips of colour and shiny buttons. The outside jacket pockets are false and placed asymmetrically to confuse evil spirits, whilst those of the waistcoat, though not seen, are embroidered and appliquéd with protective devices.

Men's trouser pockets are also highlighted with distracting pattern. In most of the Carpathians – Poland, Rumania, Slovakia – and also in Alpine regions, the pocket slits from front waist are decorated with floral patterning or couched braiding. In Rumania they are known as *feresti* – 'windows' – and are embroidered with the same patterns as those which surround house windows to protect the occupants against demons and illness with their magic powers.

In northern Syria women made wedding trousers for their husbands in heavy indigo cotton, embroidering zigzag patterning round the side pockets and also on the cuffs. Their own coats of indigo have one side pocket ornately decorated with embroidery and appliqué, while the other side of the skirt is left plain.

Most dramatic of all embroidery around pockets is that of the enormously wide cotton robes made and worn by the Hausa men of northern Nigeria. A large rectangular pocket is covered with embroidery and then applied on the left side of the chest, the patterns being continued across to the right and up around the neck to the centre back. The stitchery is most often of open chain and eyelet, traditionally in cotton thread or wild silk. The designs, drawn by specialist men, combine interlacing patterns of Islamic inspiration, long triangles known as 'knives', criss-crossed squares and the indigenous motifs of spirals, ornate crosses and open angular shapes found on other decorative arts including body scarification.

Patterns

Embroidered patterns deemed effective against evil spirits are those also chosen for amulets and jewelry, for tattooing, for felts, and as decorative devices on buildings, particularly at thresholds. Many are geometric whose origin lies in ancient mythology: the triangle, zigzag, rhomb, labyrinth, crescent, circle, 8-pointed star and cross. From the animal world fish, hands, eyes and horns have tremendous power. Birds, especially cocks, are often associated with horns as protective clan symbols. They are usually paired – in Bulgaria they are placed across the front neck in order to form the pattern of a cross.

The force of a pattern is strengthened by doubling or repeating it, by positioning it strategically and by adding protective materials such as tassels or shells. On shifts of Eastern European countries formerly under Ottoman rule a small single unfinished pattern, set asymmetrically or alone, is especially powerful. Symbolizing the continuity of life, it is of more ancient origin than the Islamic desire to leave something imperfect. Patterns forming a border are also frequently left with a gap.

Geometric patterns

The triangle, zigzag and rhomb The triangle has many associations. It defines the female sexual region and thus evokes fertility, its sharp corners have the power to blind the evil eye and it symbolizes the power of the trinity in many religions both established (as in Christianity) and pagan (as in ancient Slav mythology with its three-headed deities). It is still an amulet for people and animals alike, from India to Morocco. In a row it forms zigzags or chevrons, symbols of water and of the snake, frequently depicted on prehistoric pottery; doubled it forms a rhomb (an oblique-angled parallelogram), another fertility symbol and a common protective brickwork pattern on the houses of northern Europe. One of the meanings of the Greek word *rhombus* is 'magic circle'.

In embroidery the triangle is a ubiquitous pattern, used especially as a zigzag row along the edge of a garment, often in appliquéd material with added stitchery. Such edgings are common, for example, on the clothing of the Lapps, on Palestinian dresses and on the headgear of many countries, such as that of the men of the mountain villages of Galicia in northern Spain, whose black wool hoods topped with three red tassels have red zigzag felt edgings and red and green zigzags embroidered across the forehead.

The triangle is the leitmotif of the embroidered costume of the Akha hill tribes of northern Thailand and Burma. Their villages are guarded by sacred gates and wooden posts supporting huge triangles of wood and painted zigzags, against 'hawks and wildcats, leopards and tigers, illness and plague, leprosy and epilepsy, vampires and weretigers, and all other bad and wicked things'. Their ritual triangular swings tower above their villages.

Circles and their derivations The circle and spiral – potent symbols of the cosmic force of the sun and moon and of the motion and rejuvenation of the wheel – also offer protection from evil spirits, as do their derivations, such as the crescent, 8-pointed star, swastika, cross within a circle and the labyrinth.

A circle within a circle often has the appearance of an eye. On the bodice fronts of the dresses of Bethlehem and Jerusalem four such circles known as 'angels' eyes' are embroidered around a medallion, surrounded by as many as eighteen borders forming a frame. The circles are reputed to protect from the evil eye. The frame, ostensibly to prevent them escaping, consists of a complex series of wavy lines, often enclosing small flower heads and rows of black, white and pink fishbone and tiny satin stitch.

The most common motifs of neolithic and Bronze-Age pottery of Europe are the geometric patterns associated with pagan cults: the 'running dog', scrolls, triangles, chevrons and zigzags, as on this Bronze-Age pot of 1300 BC from Videlles, Essonne, in France.

141

Above the panel are two small sinuous birds, believed to bring good luck.

The evil eye as a pattern in itself forms a dramatic back to the hooded brown woollen cloaks of the Berbers of the High Atlas in Morocco. It is inserted as a woven section of red wool above the hem, stretching right across the back of the garment, and diamond, triangular and zigzag patterns are added in supplementary weft weaving and embroidery, with loose threads left hanging to create movement.

Variations of the circle have protective powers. The spiral – a pattern that was trodden on to ancient ground to sanctify it before a city was built, and is still marked on thresholds and floors from Bangladesh to Czechoslovakia – is a distinct motif of felt carpets and is frequent in embroidery. It features, with horns and swastikas, on the embroidered clothing of the region of Zadar in Yugoslavia.

The 8-pointed star is one of the most common motifs of all but does not always have protective powers. It was, however, embroidered on the lappets of *beniqa*, Algerian pixie-hoods mentioned by Haedo in the seventeenth century as being worn by all Muslim women in Algiers, specifically to repel evil spirits. These bonnets had two long lappets which were wound round plaits, with the embroidery at the bottom or massed on the part covering the head.

The square was considered a magical source of protection by the Chinese, Indians, Arabs and Persians. The rectangular and latticed labyrinth patterns embroidered in sober monochrome on the front of women's blouses in the village of Navalcan in Spain were, too, considered to have magical properties.

Associated with the circle as symbol of the sun is the *boteh*, *kairi* or paisley shape that held the soul bird as the sun held the soul and was believed to have powers against witchcraft. It developed in Mughal India from Persian sources, and then passed into European textiles, but with no lingering supernatural associations.

The circle enclosing a cross is one of the patterns of the embroidered *shabraks* of Pazyryk and is a powerful symbol. It appears on the costume of the Tchuvash and also on that of Bulgaria, where many patterns are shared with medieval monuments and with runic script.

The motif of the cross itself is used with the power of Christianity but also with its more ancient pagan associations as a pattern against evil. Tracing a cross on an object cuts it and sacrifices it; crossing oneself asks for protection; crossing another takes away their influence; crossroads disperse evil as the spirits are disorientated; and the cross is also a talisman and a chest pendant favoured above all others.

Numbers

Numbers are also effective against witchcraft. In the peasant costume of Europe rhythms can be discerned in patterns, which can be simply single or double; in threes and sevens, or multiples thereof; or in twelves, and these repetitions appear persistently on coifs, costume and jewelry. Three is interpreted as the Trinity and seven the gifts of the Holy Spirit, but they undoubtedly stem from earlier sources. The bonnets of Sarthe in France, for example, have seven flowers embroidered on the crown as a protective device.

Hand and fish

Both hand and fish feature in palaeolithic art, the one symbolizing the female pudendum, the other the phallus. Though their symbolic meaning is now lost, their potency against the evil eye remains. The fish shape as amuletic jewelry is popular from eastern Asia to Europe, protecting and bringing good luck. The hand is chosen as a motif in Islamic countries, the five fingers being associated with the five tenets of Islam. The hand can be raised palm outwards, where it opposes evil spirits with the reproductive power of the female, or palm inwards where it constitutes an obstacle deflecting the evil eye downwards. Raised hands on scarecrows in many lands kept not only birds but also harmful spirits away from fields.

In embroidery it is particularly in the costume of Tunisia that the pattern of hand and fish predominate, especially on marriage robes. The hand is often stylized into an almost floral pattern, or has an eye in the palm, a design which would originally have more closely resembled the female genitalia. The fish is sometimes embroidered with a horn shape in its mouth, intended to pierce the evil eye. Both hand and fish often merge into a general overall pattern and are hardly discernible.

Materials

Embroidery and jewelry almost merge in the materials associated with stitchery in its protective and magical role. The earliest jewelry – holding talismanic powers and denoting kinship and social standing – stemmed from the natural world: teeth, claws, bones, hair, feathers, shells, stones. Linen and felt, indigo and incense, even the act of spinning, have similar magical associations. Still today the materials whose own potency against spirits enhances that of embroidery come often from ecological sources: cowrie shells are the supreme example. These, with scraps of felt, tassels of hair or wool, pompoms, mirrors, coins, beads, objects that tinkle or flutter and gaudy colours, put evil spirits to rout. Often the choice depends on what is available – a local shell or beetle wing – but sometimes goods are traded over great distances. By their very nature many of these materials do not strictly constitute embroidery but are so frequently found associated with it that their role cannot be ignored. The juxtaposition goes far back in time.

When Howard Carter first shone his torch into the inner chamber of Tutankhamun's tomb in 1922 and gazed on fabulous treasures of gold and lapis he may scarcely have noticed a small linen headkerchief. Dating from about 1350 BC it combines embroidery with prophylactic materials. It is decorated with chain stitch and covered with appliquéd circles, strips, small rectangles and snakes, with added metal discs, flat circular beads and tassels.

A later example is a Chinese silk embroidery of pheasants on branches, found among the Pazyryk textiles. Probably taken to Siberia by a Chinese princess given in marriage, it had been made into a saddle lining by the semi-nomadic 'barbarians' of the Altai, who had added around its edge a primitive decoration of inlaid gold and tinfoil with a fringe of large tassels of hair and wool and little hanging bags.

Cowries and other shells

Most powerful of all talismanic additions to embroidery is the cowrie. The shell of the mollusc *Cypraea moneta* found in the Indian Ocean around the archipelago of the Maldives – a string of atolls south of India – the cowrie, resembling as it does the female vulva, is universally appreciated for its magical powers. It was also widely accepted as currency: it functioned as coinage in ancient China, where cowries have been found in Stone-Age graves, and still served as money in the early twentieth century in West Africa.

In Ceylon and Bengal, cowries were traded for rice, from whence Arab merchants took them to the Red Sea and the Mediterranean, and by camel across to West Africa – a camel could carry up to 150,000 shells. In 1887 a French officer named Caron visited Mali and noted that two and a half kilos of rice were worth one hundred cowries, and a sheep five thousand. Cowries accompany embroidery on much royal regalia of Africa and also on masks and musical instruments. Arabs and Persians also traded cowries up the Volga river to Siberia, where they feature on the embroidered costume of the Finno-Ugric people. Here they are known as *vzhova* (adder) as they resemble a snake's head, and were as valuable as silver.

Other examples of their value are given by Ibn Battúta, the Moroccan traveller who toured the Islamic world in the fourteenth century. When he called at the Maldives, the Wazir presented him with a hundred thousand cowries for his expenses. He was later given two slave girls, some pieces of silk and a casket of jewels. He sold some of the jewels for cowries with which he hired a vessel to take him to Bengal.

Cowries feature particularly on accessories and are widely used on embroidered headdresses and animal trappings from India to the Middle East. They are generally stitched in mass or in lines, but sometimes form a symbolic design such as in the ritual textiles of the Naga and the peoples of western Sumatra.

Various shells and seeds are often substituted for cowries. The belts of the Akha women of Thailand, for example, are decorated with solid rows of cowries, but if the woman is poor they are replaced by Job's tear seeds. These seeds are the outside shells of the tropical grass *Coix lachryma jobi*, which are left in the embers of a fire for two weeks so that they turn the desired shade of white. The only other hill tribe who use them are the Sgaw Karen whose married women embroider their blouses with the seeds, and with stitchery in geometric pattern.

Du Halde, who travelled to China in the early eighteenth century, noted that the Miao people of the south west wore jackets with the seams loaded with the smallest shells they could find in the seas around Yunnan and the local lakes. In Mexico shells and feathers were used both as jewelry and on garments of pre-Hispanic design, such as the Aztec men's cloaks (*tilmatli*).

Coins

There has always been a persistent belief in the power of coins to heal and to avert evil so that they have often been pierced to make jewelry and to be stitched on to clothing. They are used in conjunction with embroidery in many parts of the world.

Coins feature particularly on headdresses. Skullcaps decorated with coins were part of the Iron-Age dress of the Finno-Ugric and Turkic peoples of Central Russia and a distinction is still made between areas of Russia where headgear is a coin cap and hanging scarf and others where the stiffened beaded headdress known generally as *kakoshnik* is worn. In Ottoman countries headscarves, caps and face masks are edged with coins.

The custom of a woman wearing her dowry wealth as jewelry has led to coins also being frequently incorporated with embroidery on the fronts of dresses, one special coin often being strategically placed at the base of the neck opening. The Lahu, Akha and Lisu hill tribes of Thailand also use coins, together with silver discs and dangles, on their headgear and festive jackets. The Akha women wear sashes so heavily weighted at the ends with embroidery, coins, buttons, beads and tassels that as they squat the ends fall between their legs, affording protective covering.

There are many substitutes for coins, including silver discs, old bottle tops, bits of zips and lead shot. Buttons are especially common, mother of pearl or white shirt buttons being favourites.

Beads

Beads were also used as currency – the *wampum* beads of the North American Indian are but one example. As jewelry they decorated the mummies of ancient Egypt and as rosaries they figure in the Catholic, Buddhist, Hindu and Islamic religions.

When used in a prophylactic manner combined with embroidery – as opposed to comprising articles made entirely of beads – they are arranged in much the same way as shells and coins, edging an article or pattern or else placed individually in a strategic position. They are usually of glass and are white, blue or coral/red. The cloths used to cover precious textiles by the nomadic peoples of Central Asia, such as the Uzbek, are usually edged in beads of white – also chosen by the tribal peoples of Kohistan to outline the patterns on their clothing.

Blue beads are associated with the power of the eye: a modern Turkish shawl will have just one blue bead hidden in the fringe at the precise centre of the back. They are chosen by the Hazara of Afghanistan to edge purses and tobacco pouches. Many headdresses, and also amulets and charms, contain blue and coral beads.

Throughout the Mediterranean world coral is believed to ensure an abundant milk supply in women and therefore frequently decorates infants' clothing, or perhaps babies' rattles in the form of a red or coral-coloured bead or a piece of coral itself, whose shape symbolizes the power of the horn, with phallic overtones. Because of this association, coral is frequently allied with the fish in Tunisian embroidery.

The Ugrian people, hunters and fishermen who live in the middle reaches of the Ob river in western Siberia, sacrifice beads to their gods and also bury their dead womenfolk in all their finest embroidered clothes, leaving on them the coins and beads and removing only the shells.

Mirror

Mirror in the Islamic world is believed to trap the evil eye, holding its reflection for ever. In Morocco women ensure their husband's fidelity by opening in front of him a lidded box lined with mirrors. As they close it again the marriage is sealed with his soul held captive. Mirror also refracts, dispersing the power of the evil eye. In 1880 Sawai Madho Singh lined his entire apartment in the city palace of Jaipur with mirrors to frighten away evil spirits. Mirror also dazzles and thus is believed to cause the evil eye to blink or even to blind it.

It is in countries that have been at some time under Islamic influence that pieces of mirror are used in embroidery. They dominate most especially in the domestic embroidery of the geographical area of north-west India into Afghanistan, and also feature on the leather and woollen garments of Central and Eastern Europe. Rows of reflective mica also figure on the ceremonial cloths of western Sumatra.

That mirrors are now merely a decorative element in Indian embroidery is indisputable; that they may not always have been so is indicated by the position in which they are placed. They form the centre of flowers and eyes for animals and birds; they divide pattern into areas and provide a focal point; they are placed strategically in a geometric design, or are isolated and accentuated by the surrounding stitches. In the festive hangings of Kathiawar they are used pictorially to depict, amongst other things, the ears of Surya the sun god, or the breasts of Radha, Krishna's consort. Mirrors almost never appear just scattered around the background, except in modern commercial embroidery.

The original material was mica which is still sometimes used. For mirrorglass large globes of blown glass are silvered on the inside and then broken into small pieces. These are still widely marketed in the villages of north-western India. The mirrors are attached by crossed stitches which are then worked over by buttonholing; otherwise a ring of thread over the mirror is fixed to the fabric by interlacing stitch.

The style of mirrorwork of each Muslim clan or Hindu sub-caste is individual. The Rajput and Ahir farming castes combine square mirrors with yellow and white interlacing in heavy cotton in strong geometric patterns, while the Rabaris mix mirrors of varied shapes in bold motifs accentuating the breasts. These castes are very religious, the earth goddess being one of their deities. They decorate their bodies with tattooing and their houses with mudwork which incorporates mirrors.

In Asia mirror was normally combined only with stitchery and not with other added decorative devices. In Hungary and in Croatia, however, woollen and leather garments, that by their cut and their vestigial sleeves betray their steppe origin, began in the nineteenth century to be decorated with pieces of mirror, along with leather discs, rosettes and tassels. The *cifraszür*, the coat owned by every young man of marriageable age in Hungary, became so overloaded with such ornaments that legal action was taken to curb excess. In Croatia it was the jackets of white or bright felted wool and the leather waistcoats that were decorated by mirror and appliquéd scraps of leather or felted wool.

In Spain the village of Montehermoso is famous for its women's high straw hats thickly covered with every protective device possible: mirrors, buttons, red cloth, bright pompoms, tassels and even horns. In Spain too small hanging purses were made for both men and women, decorated with mirror, tassels, buttons, sequins and bells.

Sequins

The sequins of Western embroidery, like gold thread and jewels, were chosen only for their expensive aura and their sparkle under the lights of church or evening ball. In peasant embroidery the shine of gold was associated with kings and gods, with dragons and serpents, and with wealth and festivity. The sparkle of sequins, however, had much in common with mirror in its protection from evil spirits.

The sequins used on the embroidered indigo dresses of Yemen, for example, are known as *lamma*, and the same word in Arabic with a long vowel means the evil eye. These sequins were made until the late 1980s in the market, the *suk*, of the capital Sana'a. An eighteenth-century report states that they were copper but on most dresses now they are brass. Punched out of the metal plate they have a distinctive central indentation. The dress front is covered to a greater or lesser degree with rows of them attached with two stitches of red cotton thread, combined with lines of white stitchery, small pieces of mother-of-pearl from the Red Sea, and triangles made of loops of brass chain.

Confusing the evil spirits

Tinkling sounds, gaudy and alternated colours, tassels and pompoms confuse the evil eye, while they also attract attention. Silver discs, bells, and even thimbles edging clothing vibrate with movement that distracts and creates a sound that in hot countries is cooling. Du Halde mentions the women of western Manchuria who wore long garments of skin with a red or green border and pieces of copper or little bells at the back hem, which gave notice of their approach. Siberian women aroused the attention of suitors with the jingling of metal sewn on to their clothes.

Edges are very frequently of fluttering tassels, often of rags, or of fringes which are a natural outcome of the weaving technique. Tassels may in some parts of the world be substitutes for feathers: the cloaks of Maori chiefs are sometimes edged with feathers and sometimes with tufts or tassels clearly in imitation. For American Indian tribes feathered headdresses and skin garments that were deeply fringed and beaded denoted social standing. In Hawaii, for example, feathers were deemed a vehicle of divine power when red or yellow, and in Central America were an integral part of pre-Conquest festive clothing.

A tassel or pompom will often be placed in precisely the same manner as a cowrie or coin at the base of the neck opening of a dress or at an embroidered pocket or other vulnerable spot. The linen trousers and shirts that the women of Lagartera in Spain made for their bridegroom are densely embroidered on shoulders, cuffs and all around a deep neck placket in bands of white and honey needleweaving with drawn threadwork. The base of the neck and of the trouser flies are adorned with tassels.

Gaudy colours, especially when alternated or when applied in little pieces of fabric, are powerful deterrents against evil. The most potent colour by far is red.

THE POWER OF RED

The symbolism of colour is complex and associations can be totally opposed: in another culture, at another point in time, the widow wears white and the bride black. The colours of the liturgy, those of joy or of jealousy, those of the clothes of kings or of chimneysweeps are imposed by society. In contrast three colours are basic to the human state: these are red, white and black. Though interpretations of their symbolism may vary, white traditionally denotes purity and the celestial, and recalls the potency of human milk and semen, while black, associated with excreta and earth, denotes decay. Though both black and white are used symbolically in costume they play no similar role in embroidery.

Red is the most powerful, the most vibrant, the most exhilarating of colours: it is the blood of life and of death. As such it is also ambiguous: life, fire, the sun and power are counterbalanced by sacrifice and death. Red threads and fabrics are associated with spirit worship and demons, with youth and marriage, with talismanic charms and secret powers. It is the predominant colour in all tribal and peasant embroidery, but is used in two entirely different ways – to protect and to mark.

Protection   In its protective role red is most commonly deployed as fabric appliquéd on vulnerable areas such as seams, edges and over the breasts. The material will generally be more expensive than that of the garment and often imported: red flannel, silk and, in linen-producing areas, fine cotton. It will often be superimposed with decorative embroidery and strengthened by cowries, bells, tassels and mirror. Patterns will be the symbolic ones of the cross, zigzags, triangles, circles, diamonds and squares.

Early examples are the linen shift found at Pazyryk, dating from about the fourth century BC, with red thread couched on all its seams, widening at the neck and wrists into a braid; the mummy wrappings of Paracas from about the same period with borders of red embroidery; and the clothes discovered in the Coppergate diggings at York, dating from the tenth or eleventh century when Jorvik was a Viking capital, which appear to have been edged with red silk ribbons, emphasizing the neck and cuffs.

Geographically, red decoration on clothing is common to many societies though interpretation of the power of red and the right to wear it vary; among the Naga, for example, only a man who has killed is entitled to red.

In Africa the Benin chiefs of Nigeria wear red cloth as ceremonial court dress to protect themselves and their king from evil spirits, while other tribes associate red with achievement. The Ful of Senegal stitch a small piece of red fabric at the nape and centre forehead of their caps. It is also the prerogative of young girls – a cloth with a red stripe is worn in Nigeria for betrothal rites, and the Masai of Kenya decorate young girls' skin skirts with red ochre. Red also relates to death: in Nigeria burial cloths of red are displayed on the roof of a hut where an eminent man has died, while in Madagascar burial cloths are known as *mena* (red) even when that colour no longer predominates but is replaced by an embroidered edge.

In the Far East the Ainu of Japan notch the hems of their gowns, binding the slit with red, as they do the base of the neck opening. The Dyak of Borneo appliqué red flannel on men's ornamental jackets, as people do in Sumatra where figurines of the dead are also wrapped in red cloth. Babies in Hong Kong were swaddled in embroidered red cloths with mirror stuck on their forehead to protect them: in the 1920s only seventy-two out of a thousand lived beyond a year. Married women of the Sgaw Karen tribe of northern Thailand and Burma embroider their blouses with red and with Job's tear seeds, inserting a deep band of red fabric along the bottom. With these blouses they wear tie-dye skirts, which they make by tying the cloth with red threads. As they associate these with spirit worship they dye the cloth in the forest where they cannot be seen. The Blue Hmong appliqué red on to clothing and baby carriers; the White Hmong place a red fabric cross at the back of a woman's jacket after the curing ceremony when a shaman has evicted from her body the offending spirits that made her ill.

In India vermilion is a sacred colour, decorating animistic shrines. It is considered auspicious and marriage textiles are predominantly of red fabric or decorated in red. The protective qualities of red are strong:

account books begin with a red swastika, red thread around the wrist makes demons impotent, sweets wrapped in red cloth are placed at crossroads to thwart evil spirits.

In Russia costume is decorated overwhelmingly in red – the word 'red' in early Russian is synonymous with beauty. The shifts of the Tcheremiss and Mordu of Siberia have every seam and edge and the eye-motifs over the breast appliquéd in red, with beads and sequins added. The ritual towels of the Ukraine have a plain red band, considered sacred in pagan belief.

In Eastern Europe red dominates all embroidered costume and is believed to have magic properties, effective against witches. Yugoslavian red felted wool is embroidered and appliquéd on to the woollen sleeveless coats, called *zubun*, of Serbia and the jackets of Bosnia. In the Dinaric mountains it is the linen shifts that have red cotton appliquéd on edges, and at the base of the mandarin collar a snippet of red fabric or a tassel is placed. In Hungary red leather appliqué was the earliest decoration of skin garments; the red ribbon encircling a couple at a Rumanian marriage was then used by the bride to tie her apron on Sundays; and in Bulgaria small red tassels on linen shifts or else an asymmetric pattern in red cross stitch separate from the rest of the design are deemed to have magic powers.

In Western Europe cottages in Wales were painted red to keep demons away; in the isolated Pyrenean valley of Bethmale men's jackets were embroidered with red feather stitching around all edges, along seams, pockets and over the shoulders, with appliquéd bands of black velvet decorated with red zigzags and crosses to afford protection. Italians wrap newborn babies in vests of red silk, believing it will bring luck; in Germany evil spirits were thought likely to attack newborn children before there was time to baptize them, so christening robes and covers spread over the child while it was being taken to church are heavily embroidered in red with appliquéd bands and facings that are mainly red. In 1526 Luther declared that white was not essential for christening robes, whereupon the people of Småland in southern Sweden returned to more pagan clothing and wrapped their babies in bags with red triangular edges, red fringing and appliquéd silk ribbons. These they hired from church, together with caps, for one silver krone.

Marking

Primitive man's sealing of contracts with blood, his marking of possessions, and the decorating of graves with red ochre finds an echo in the extraordinary power of red in Western European embroidery. While costume and embroideries for the home slavishly follow fashions, linen articles for the trousseau remain resolutely monogrammed and numbered in red cross stitch. This custom of marking ritual textiles in red is almost inextricably bound to the life-consuming production of home-grown, handspun, handwoven linen. Replaced by purchased cotton the bottom drawer linen of continental Europe is still marked in red.

The home production of linen in Europe was a life-consuming task, each stage of which was imbued with ritual. Trousseau textiles included embroidered shirts and shifts and household linens marked in red cross stitch.

In Spain and Portugal linen shirts, made by the bride for her groom, are marked in red cross stitch below the neck placket, which is heavily embroidered in white. Red tassels were almost always added. Those of Caceres and Salamanca have the man's name or initials, those of Segovia the couple's names and marriage date and those of Guimarães in Portugal a sentimental word like *amizade* or *amor*. Sometimes the lettering has no meaning as the women embroiderers were of course illiterate. Such marking by red cross stitch initials is common on the women's linen chemises of Abruzzo in Italy and of Switzerland. In the Black Forest region of Germany married men's shirts were worked with symbols such as hearts, stars and zigzags in red, and the bachelors' in white. Their braces, similarly embroidered, were reversed in colour – red for bachelors and white for married men. A newborn Bulgarian baby's shift, ritualistically made and symbolizing the child's skin, is always marked with red stitches around the neck as a first statement of the child's passage into the human race.

Western European household linens for the trousseau are marked with red cross stitch, usually by a monogram, and are frequently also numbered. As laundry was a social activity at river bank or village washhouse such marking served in addition a practical purpose, in the same way that bread baked in a communal oven was stamped with distinctive symbols to identify its owner. The marking of linen was the motivation for the myriad red alphabet samplers of the schoolgirls of Europe.

HIGH DAYS AND HOLY PLACES
High Days

Textiles have always played a significant ritual role, even in the earliest societies, being offered or exchanged as gifts, or else burned or buried at the major events in life, whether religious, military or social. The high days for embroidered textiles in the human life-cycle – when the magical power of decoration on dress is invoked to protect from evil spirits – are the rites of passage: birth, marriage, death. In most societies, a period – either of vulnerability, as for the newborn or the spirit of the recently deceased, or of uncleanliness, as for the new mother – was set at forty days, after which some ceremony involving embroidered clothing was held to signal the return to normal life. In the astrological religion of Babylon forty, together with three and seven, was considered a perfect number, linked to the completion of the lunar cycle.

The role of embroidered clothing in celebrating the passage from one human condition to another is exemplified by the linen shirt or shift of Europe. Representing the human skin in an analogy of the regeneration of the scales of mythological creatures, it acts as a marker through life. It is a ritual and sacred object, its decoration the transference of the tribal signs of tattooing into embroidery, its cut the simple joining of loom widths with nothing wasted. In Rumania the small piece cut out for the neck is thrown with incantations into a fast-flowing river; in Bulgaria the linen for the new baby's first shirt is not cut but torn out by beating with stones. In almost every society from the stitching round the neck of the baby's shirt – in Bulgaria always in red thread – the embroidery reaches its richest and heaviest for the young and most particularly for marriage, to become more subdued and end as a simple neck border in old age. In most parts of the world people were buried in their marriage shirt or entire costume, ostensibly so that their partner could recognize them in the next world, but on a magico-religious plane to identify them as a human being.

Birth

Until the birth of her first child the mother was considered vulnerable to evil, belonging neither to her own family, nor yet to her husband's, and in many countries she kept on for everyday wear her marriage costume and amuletic jewelry. On giving birth she was normally considered unclean and new baby and mother were protected by embroidery and other devices against illness and the mother's own uncleanliness. In Bulgaria she was known as *lehusa* and her shirt was decorated with a needle threaded with red, pieces of garlic and blue beads around the neck to keep her own evil spirits within her and prevent others from entering. On the fortieth day these decorations were left on a tree and she was taken to church.

In Czechoslovakia, where as many as twenty or thirty people lived in one room and concepts of hygiene were not understood, an embroidered bedcurtain known as a *kutnice* protected the mother, separating her from the room, a magical separation that was enhanced by objects placed around the curtain: herbs, garlic, strips of red and green cloth, needles and knives. The patterns embroidered on the curtain were symbolic, deriving from both ancient cult and Christianity, and often included open drawn threadwork, enabling the mother to see into the room. For six weeks mother and baby were totally confined and then attended a cleansing ceremony in church, the 'Churching of Women' of the Christian faith. In some villages the mother went shrouded in the *kutnice*, in others she wore her marriage stole or else a special cloth was embroidered.

Similar purification ceremonies were performed at the hammam, the public baths of Ottoman countries, also involving embroidered cloths both for the mother and for the ritual washing of the baby. In Turkey the groom's mother would rent the hammam for forty days and the bride would be bathed and her hair unplaited, with towels embroidered for the occasion.

Symbolic embroideries also assisted labour. In the Ukraine the cloth used the previous year to bless the *packa* (Easter bread) was tied to a beam above the mother's bed for her to pull on; in Tunisia it was the marriage belt that was so used. In Thrace her apron was thrown over her stomach.

At the birth it was often the grandmother's role to begin embroideries to which she would devote most of her time until the child married, as in

The protective role of the bedcurtain confining mother and baby for forty days after childbirth is often augmented by devices such as garlic and knives or, in the case of this curtain from Poprad, Slovakia, a display of trousseau linen shifts.

In Germany, a child was prepared for baptism by being wrapped in a cloth decorated in red; in Grisons, Switzerland, the protection was afforded by the symbolic tree of life with the fertility motifs of carnation and tulip.

Hungary. In the Punjab at the birth of a boy the paternal grandmother began the *bagh*, the embroidered cloth that he would give his bride.

In China, about forty days after the birth of a male child, the first ceremonial hair-cutting takes place, at which the mother is entitled to wear the embroidered jacket she was given as a bride by her parents. The baby's first hair-cutting had magical significance in many other countries, as the hair was believed to retain the spiritual strength of the person.

Marriage

Almost everywhere the event at which embroidery plays its major ritual role is marriage. Customs are immensely varied, but universal themes are common to most countries: the preparation by the girl throughout her childhood of items for her trousseau; the significance of her ability as an embroideress in gaining a husband; the public display of the embroidered trousseau to demonstrate her skill and the textile wealth she is bringing to the marriage; the use of embroidery on costume to mark the change in status, particularly of the bride; the ritual offering of embroidered gifts by both parties; the use of embroidered cloths in the wedding ceremonies and, above all, the quasi-sacred status of the marriage shirt or dress.

Trousseau embroideries mainly consist of a lifetime's supply of clothing for the bride and gifts (such as the embroidered betel bag given by the Banjara bride to her husband, the linen shirts made for him by European girls, the tobacco pouches, purses and caps made by the Syrian bride for the men of her family to lessen their grief when she leaves home, or covers such as the one the Korean groom ties round a small wooden goose to give the bride's mother as a token of his fidelity). Embroideries that feature in the wedding ceremonies, such as cloths for the couple to sit on, to decorate the bridal room, or to cover ritual articles – the coconuts and water used in some Indian marriages for example – are also included, together with one of the most important items, linen for the marriage bed.

In Eastern Europe sets of linen were embroidered by the girl for the symbolic bed, set in the corner of the 'best' room and never actually slept in. Embroideries stacked up to the ceiling were normally seen only by the family but when the girl was of marriageable age, they were shown to others, even displayed outside the home. On marriage they were carried through the village to the bridegroom's house. The linen was changed for childbirth, and at time of death, when it was put on the funeral bier and again carried for all to see. Trousseau linen remained the property of the woman and was handed down through the female line. If a woman had no daughter it was buried with her or reclaimed by her family.

Embroidery was also significant in the lives of young men. In Hungary every young man of marriageable age owned a *szür*, a coat of fulled wool with floral embroidery on its large square collar and edges, often acquired as his first wages. He would wear it all through courtship, at his marriage and afterwards for festive occasions. The bridegrooms of Mezőkövesd wore

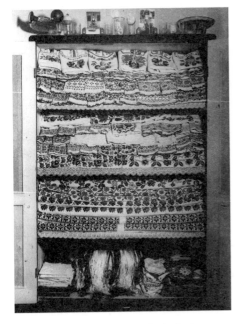

Throughout Eastern Europe the bride, however poor, would have an immense store of embroidered linen for her trousseau. Some she would have spent most of her childhood making and some would have been inherited from or made by her mother.

The bridegroom's shirt was an important element of embroidered trousseau linen. Most spectacular are those of Mezőkövesd where a boy was given his shirt on becoming a young man. At death his shroud was made from the sleeves of the shirt he had worn as a bridegroom.

floral aprons and shirts with immensely wide embroidered sleeves made for them by their bride. In Montenegro young men were only allowed to wear embroidered clothes after marriage when they were considered fit to go fighting. The young men of Minho in Portugal would buy at fairs sweetheart hankies embroidered in red with some sentimental device, to bestow on the girl they loved. These had the same significance as a ring, ending the engagement if they were returned. Among the hill tribes of Thailand young men, especially the Lisu, carried elaborate 'courting' bags decorated with beads, stitchery, tassels, strips of cloth and silver ornaments.

The consummation of marriage brings its own customs involving embroideries. In many countries the shift or a cloth stained with blood on the wedding night is displayed by the mother to prove her daughter's virginity. In North Africa on the third or seventh day the ceremony of the belt marks the transition of the bride from a goddess-like creature shrouded in embroidered robes to a domesticated woman. Her wide marriage clothing hid her body from evil spirits who might make her sterile before the marriage was consummated. When this danger is past she puts on a heavy woollen shawl – in eastern Tunisia dyed half indigo and half henna – with a densely embroidered centre strip, clasping it round the waist with a belt. It is later worn over the head without a belt.

Death

Burial In many societies textiles – not necessarily embroidered – were buried with the dead as provision for the afterlife or as ritual gifts. Though embroidery was occasionally done specifically for burial clothes, more frequently the marriage shirt or entire costume becomes the shroud at death. Often each partner is buried with half the cloth that tied them at marriage and was then torn in two.

It was a tradition among Turkic peoples for a man who died in battle to be buried in his clothes; otherwise, as they symbolize the man, they were tied to a pole on the burial mound or replaced by a piece of crudely embroidered felt. In many societies it was customary too for offerings of embroideries, or bits of rag or animal skin, to be tied to a bush near the tomb.

In Indonesia most ornamental textiles are buried with the dead, but few are embroidered. Only in the women's sarongs of Lampung in southern Sumatra is embroidery the dominant technique, and in those of the east of Sumba island where decoration is appliquéd. Both these areas are wealthy, the first trading in pepper and the second in horses.

Sumba chiefs were required to bury fifty to a hundred textiles with the corpse and to donate others to guests. Such decorated textiles were once the prerogative of the nobility and the women's skirts, known as *lau hada*, decorated with beads and imported nassa shells were both an important part of the dowry and also served as grave gifts, buried with their owner.

The design is always an upright figure with arms raised in worship and with exaggerated sexual parts. Between the legs is a lizard, symbol of fecundity, and around the figure are fish or crustaceans such as crabs and lobsters – denoting rebirth as they regenerate their limbs – and crocodiles whom several Sumba clans believe to be their ancestors. Cotton tufting separates the motifs.

The most famous textiles of the Lampung area of southern Sumatra are the ritual weavings known as 'ship of the dead' cloths. Similar patterns are worked on one type of the women's embroidered sarongs, the *tapis* that come from the mountainous region. They consist of bands of ikat alternated with embroidered bands of ships bearing trees and people, worked in satin stitch in cream, brown and blue silk with the patterns outlined. Another type has embroidery of weird shapes resembling cells under a microscope. Those of the Abung of the south and south east are worked in couched gold thread with geometric patterns or motifs of people and animals. Those of the Kauer on the far west coast bear hundreds of small mirrors or pieces of mica, and were worn with jackets embroidered with mirror and shells. A girl could only marry once she had completed her *tapis* and they were worn at all rites of passage.

Funeral In many European countries embroideries were made specifically for the funeral, or for the religious ceremony forty days after death: in the village of Csokoly in Hungary girls would start to embroider sheets and pillows in red for their own funeral bed, and at about forty years of age they would begin a new set in yellow; in many parts of Sweden and Norway it was customary for the coffin to be displayed in the home before the procession set out and richly embroidered cloths would be laid over it; it was a Spanish custom to place funeral mats with Christian symbols worked in dark wool over the coffin and on All Souls Day cloths embroidered with funereal motifs were spread on the church floor and candles stood on them; in the Ukraine ritual cloths were tied to crosses; and in Rumania cloths in red and black cross stitch were offered to the family and priests and worn by the pall bearers over their shoulder. They were deemed to have magic powers to protect the deceased's spirit and when hearses carried the body instead, the cloths were not abandoned but were tied to the car door handle.

At funerals of the Pwo Karen in Burma and Thailand girls carry singing shawls made from the woven red blankets that normally cover the sleeping with the fringe at the foot, but are placed with it at the head for the dead. One half of the blanket is covered with white beads in groups of three or five and a fringe of beetles' wings and bells is hung from the bottom.

Mourning Mourning generally involves sober colouring and often the reversal of garments. The custom of turning clothing inside out for mourning is recorded by Ibn Battúta who describes mourners, on the death of the son of a sultan in about 1330, wearing rough, badly stitched garments inside out for forty days. Wearing clothing inside out or reversed

155

at funerals was a recent custom in Europe and was believed to denote the disarray of the soul at death and its need of protection from magic forces. The women's jackets of Pont-Aven in Brittany are embroidered specifically for such use, their orange and yellow patterning being richly worked on the right side and more soberly on the left, the side they are fastened when the wearer is in mourning.

Headhunting Decapitation was at the root of Paracas mythology, symbolizing the role of death in sustaining life. Embroideries depict mythical feline figures, raptorial birds and round-eyed figures known as oculate beings, bearing trophy heads in baskets or as appendages to their body.

Almost three thousand years later, to the Naga tribe – a warlike people whose territory is still barred to outsiders – headhunting was a deeply symbolic practice, which even the British administration in India had difficulty in stamping out. The magical power residing in the head made it imperative to present that of a human victim at the funeral of a chief, though heads were also taken merely as a result of simple feuding or because of a more complex belief. A woman's head with abundant hair encouraged fertility and even a child's was considered a trophy. The hunters wore shawls of striped brown and black cotton with circles of cowries denoting the moon and small brocaded red squares. They were not allowed red until they had killed nor cowries until they had slain two men, when the shells were often applied in the form of a human figure, added to a circle or as a separate motif.

The same people erected monolithic stones in honour of their dead, which entailed hundreds of people dragging the stone uphill, an event for which the women would sew masses of coins on the back of their sarongs. This Herculean task was followed by feasting, after which the young men who had participated, now known as *lung-chingba*, had to live apart from their family for a year. They were then entitled to wear a shawl of dark blue cloth woven in Manipur and embroidered with quaint figures of animals, mainly in red.

The Naga would also give a series of feasts of merit, when a man would provide food for all the village. Once this had been achieved and a *mithan* (buffalo) had been slaughtered, the hunter responsible was entitled to wear cloths decorated with cowries, as were his womenfolk.

Festivities

In European peasant life 'best' or marriage clothes were worn for festivities that were mainly concerned with the seasons and the production of food and linen. Ceremonies to greet the spring often involved young girls ripe for marriage treading fields and collecting eggs, dressed in their best embroidered costume. The proportion of peasant income spent on embroideries is astounding: a poor girl, living in a shack in Hungary simple enough to take only a day to erect, could have as many as thirty or forty embroidered dresses and several hundred pieces of linen.

After haymaking, girls of Dobra Niva in Slovakia put on their best embroidered costume and present a cake to the landowner.

Richly embroidered costume was worn on any occasion that was considered social. This included churchgoing, communal work in the fields and visits to market – Eastern European women can still be seen wearing elements of embroidered costume at market. Even mundane agricultural tasks, once they were performed by a large group of peasants together, were treated as an opportunity for 'best' wear. Martha Wilmot, travelling around Russia in the early nineteenth century, comments on an occasion when several hundred peasants had gathered together to cart manure and even for this the women wore their shifts embroidered with red and their horned headdresses.

Churchgoing was at the heart of every community and the prime occasion for dressing up. Pagan rites of spring had been successfully incorporated into Easter, but cloths were still embroidered to cover baskets of eggs, fruit and bread, to be taken to church. Easter eggs in Moravia are still painted with the same patterns as those on embroidered clothing. In the early twentieth century in Mezőkövesd clothing was becoming more and more overloaded with sequins to the detriment of the embroidery, sequins which cost the peasants dear – one apron could have the value of a calf stitched on it in baubles. To save the peasants from ruin the Church stepped in and on Ash Wednesday in 1925 banned all sequins. At the Easter service the six thousand girls and young people of the town turned up at church in new embroidered clothes with patterns imitating the banned sequins. There was no question of individual choice but only of belonging to the community and establishing status by embroidery.

Religious processions are also high days for embroidered clothing in Catholic countries, including those of Central and South America. In Spain banners are hung from balconies, in other countries effigy bearers wear embroidered cloths on their shoulders.

In Jewish homes special cloths for the Sabbath table and plaited bread (*challah*) are usually embroidered with biblical quotations and religious symbols such as candles and the bread itself. At the festival of Passover, commemorating the exodus from Egypt, services are held in the home. For these, cushion covers are embroidered and also bags in which three symbolic slices of the unleavened bread (*matzah*) could be kept. Jewish embroidery is normally in the style of the country in which the people live.

Surpassing all other festive activities – its roots in the animal instincts of the human psyche – is dance. North-American Indian war dances, dances for fulfilling dreams and curing illness, Bushmen's primeval dances of the moon, and many more similar dances throughout the world, required decorated costume, be it only special beads or feathers. The dance festivals of Europe are the last repository of embroidered dress. In most a hybrid 'national costume' has been cobbled together from diverse regional styles, but gradually care is beginning to be taken to use or copy genuine old costumes, with the correct style of embroidery of the region from which each particular dance comes.

Holy Places

Holy corners

The modest town of Banske Bystrica in Czechoslovakia straggles along the flank of a hill, its streets a jumble of the shabby baroque of an outpost of the Austro-Hungarian empire and the bleak concrete of Communist rule. The front door of a typical house leads directly into a kitchen/dining/living area furnished in 1950s style, a bizarre note struck by a radio shrouded in embroidery. The second room is what used to be called in Britain until very recent years the 'front' room. Here visitors are received. The room has chests full of textiles, the housewife's heritage from her mother's trousseau and her own. A television stands on a table by the wall, with plates displayed behind. Embroidered cloths cover the TV set and are draped around the plates. This is the holy corner of the ancient Eurasian hunting societies.

The holy corner marked the entry point for spirits coming into the earthly world, and the resting place of the souls of the departed who, it was believed, returned to their homes on festive occasions. The corner is usually sited by the family dining table on the opposite side of the room from the stove. The simplest have an icon and a lamp hung across them, as in Russia. More commonly a triangular shelf fills the space, on which bread is often placed, or an egg at Easter. A newer version is a religious picture hung on the wall. There were traditionally five elements: a holy picture or statue, an embroidered linen cloth symbolizing the bands that swaddled Christ at his birth and death, something green for the tree of life, a bird linking the soul to earth, and a light denoting the presence of God. In Catholic homes the picture or statue is of the Madonna; in Orthodox households, it is an icon; amongst Muslims, where a prayer mat is unrolled on the floor for daily prayers, it is a *mihrab* or a Koran on a shelf draped with embroidery; for Jewish peoples it is the *menorah* (the seven-branched candelabrum used in the Temple and an emblem of Judaism), the *Torah*, a painted amulet or, on the eastern wall of the house, the *mizrach*, a picture that may be embroidered.

The holy corner of the home was hung with embroidered cloths, painted plates, religious pictures and often records of family rites of passage.

Gradually the five elements of the holy corner have largely been replaced in many homes by records of family rites of passage – photos of communion and marriage, diplomas, certificates of military service – and above all, by the television set. All are still draped with embroidered cloths like those hung on birch trees or in sacrificial groves. They are almost always long and narrow with embroidery at each end, usually in red cross stitch and with motifs derived from ancient cult, although north European motifs are those commonly worked on samplers: initials, dates, the tree of life and confronting birds. Similar cloths are also hung by the stove, where often the family's clothing is displayed, and in northern Europe more frequently on posts by the door, or by washbasins which, like wells, merit decoration because of the power of water. Everywhere painted plates are similarly draped, as are sources of light such as windows, candlesticks and mirrors.

Mirrors

Mirrors are hung with embroidered cloths in countries from China to Eastern Europe. The blue and white embroideries of the peasants of southwest China include hangings for mirrors; in Syria *mikhala*, small shield-like panels designed to hang over mirrors to avert the evil eye are embroidered in small zigzag patterns devised to dazzle, with the usual addition of tassels, blue beads, coins and sometimes patchwork; in Eastern Europe mirrors are covered at death. In Tetouan, Morocco, a mirror hung opposite the marital bed is draped with an embroidered cloth for forty days after the wedding, bearing a design of a pyramid of pomegranates at each end.

Altars

Many homes have temporary altars: at Easter in Minho, Portugal, for example, the priest would go round all the houses blessing them, and in each a small altar would be made of a table draped with a cloth embroidered in red cross stitch with Christian symbols and even declarations of fidelity to the king. The nomadic Banjara of India make an altar by placing a small embroidered cloth edged with cowries on a table or chest and laying on it five balls of dough, one in each corner and one in the centre. The *rumals* of Chamba, embroidered with mythological scenes, were hung behind a cult picture to form an altar.

Thresholds

The threshold of house or tent is sacred, the place whose decoration safeguards the home and its inhabitants. In ancient Egypt a winged globe with snakes either side was placed above the lintel as a protection from evil; Friar William of Rubruck, travelling to Central Asia in 1253 commented on the hangings depicting vines, trees, birds and beasts over doorways, and Carpini, ambassador to the Mongol Great Khan in 1246, mentioned felt images of men on each side of tent doorways; O'Donovan cites the Scythian practice of sewing near doorways a square piece of linen making a pocket to receive the bounties of wandering spirits. Today in many countries sacred symbols – swastikas, fish, solar circles, crosses – are common above doors; the Bedouin tent has red rags tied at the entrance, the Mongolian *yurt* a criss-cross pattern of red fabric; in Bengal the threshold floor is decorated with the same symbols in rice flour (as thanksgiving for the safety of the house) that are embroidered on *kanthas*; in the streets of Luxembourg doors carved with the tree of life, sun discs, crosses and the arrows of Saint Sebastian are still to be seen.

Embroideries are commonly hung around doorways in a geographical swathe starting with those of China, through the *suzanis* of Central Asia to the appliquéd portières of Egypt. In Jewish homes the *mezuzah*, a parchment inscribed with a prayer from Deuteronomy to be recited daily, must be placed on the doorpost: in North Africa it hangs in an embroidered case.

The threshold of a home is a sacred place. Those of Bengal are decorated with symbols in rice flour that are also embroidered on kanthas.

The Calcutta pavement dweller hangs at the hub of 'home' an embroidered cloth.

In many countries, however, it is the spot right opposite the threshold that forms the living core of the house and it is here that embroideries are displayed. This is often where the family altar or the best bed, used only for marriage or occasionally guests, will be sited. This bed almost everywhere carries the finest embroideries of the household – covers, valances, pillows, curtains. Other embroideries might be hung on a beam opposite the threshold or perhaps the household's wealth in textiles might be piled here and covered with an embroidery, as the *dharkala* quilts of Gujarat. Even a Calcutta pavement dweller hangs an embroidery at the hub of 'home'.

On the Dodecanese islands it is on bedcurtains or on the doorways of bed-tents, rather than of the house, that embroidery is concentrated, with figurative motifs on the gable, particularly birds but also the goddess, stags, boats and two-headed eagles.

Precious objects

Precious objects afforded protection by embroidery range from babies and camels to guns and spoons. Each society has its own priorities.

In sixteenth- and seventeenth-century Turkey, for example, the turban, worn as a public declaration of adherence to Islam, was a symbolic garment placed on a carved wooden shelf when it was not being worn, where specially embroidered cloths, *kavur örtüsü*, covered it. These were of pale linen worked in double darning stitch with tulips and artichokes, palmettes, or *çintemani*. When the fez, a simple hat without symbolic meaning, replaced the turban, covers were no longer embroidered. Once a turban was wound it was never undone and on the death of an important person it was placed on his tomb. The sultans' caftans were also wrapped in similar embroidered cloths called *bohça* when not worn, and on their death were stored in the treasury inside a number of such cloths.

The custom of wrapping precious articles or clothing in decorated cloths is of nomadic origin, but is practised in other societies. The *kanthas* of Bengal protect all manner of precious things, such as books, the Koran, musical instruments, money, betel nuts, mirrors, combs and toilet articles. Their making is a ritual activity: for Muslim women Friday is an auspicious day to begin, while for Hindus it is a Tuesday. Patterns vary with district and purpose but are conventionally a central lotus with a tree of life in each corner, with motifs of everyday household articles – rice huskers, betel cutters or earrings, which are a symbol of the married state – scattered over the rest of the cloth. The long narrow kanthas for the women's personal toiletries, known as *arshilata*, have floral or linear patterning, often with red edges and a red tassel at each corner.

Afghan women embroider covers for almost everything, especially guns, which enable their menfolk to show others the needlework skills of their bride. The Baluch embroider bags for their spoons; the Chinese, purses and cases for spectacles and fans to hang from a belt; and Jewish people, bags for the men's embroidered prayer shawls (*tallit*).

continued on page 177

THE MAGICAL SOURCE OF PROTECTION

EVIL SPIRITS

134   Dress cuff, Bethlehem-style sleeve on Beit Dajan dress, Palestine. Embroidery is strategically positioned on garments to protect the body from evil spirits. Edgings and seams are particularly important and a common device in many parts of the world is to decorate them with alternate colouring.

135   Dress, Baluch, Pakistan. Patterning is concentrated at the shoulder, over the breasts and sexual area and on all edges and seams. Even when protective ornamentation almost covers the entire garment, the areas of embroidery never intermingle but are always clearly defined.

136   Man's robe, Nigeria. Whereas the front neck placket is usually one of the most decorated parts of a garment, the back neck, particularly of men's clothing, often carries a strong ornamental motif. This is common, not only in West Africa but also in India.

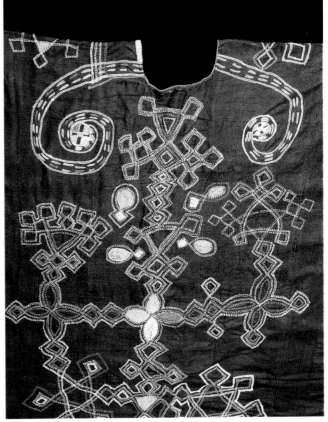

137 Woman's robe, Sana'a, Yemen. A frequent protective device is some intricate pattern worked inside the hem of a garment so that with movement a dazzling effect is achieved. Sequins that sparkle and triangular amulets increase the power of this design hidden under the back hem.

138 Blouse, choli, Rajput caste, Kutch, India. A source of life for the newborn baby, breasts are protected by heavy embroidery on the women's clothing of many cultures. In Europe a separate embroidered stomacher fulfilled the same purpose.

139 Apron, Bosača, Slovakia. The European apron was symbolic and not practical: it protected the body rather than the garment below, which was normally left plain where the apron would cover it. Ritual associations of the apron are legion.

140 Child's cap, Sana'a, Yemen. The head is protected by the potent amulet of a triangle.

141 Woman's dress. Uzbek Lakai, Afghanistan. Pockets were strengthened and decorated with embroidery. They were often placed asymmetrically to confuse the evil eye.

142 Woman's blouse, Pieštany, Slovakia. The sleeves of European peasant costume were frequently a ritual object associated with marriage. They were usually of fine fabric or were intricately pleated or heavily embroidered.

143 Woman's bolero, Bosnia, Yugoslavia. Patterns deemed effective against the evil eye often originated in ancient cults: the ram's horn motif from palaeolithic hunting societies is one. This jacket has a powerful red edging to the neck, and, on the front, a small isolated asymmetric pattern embroidered in dazzling silks.

144 Woman's scarf, Gabès, southern Tunisia. In the Islamic world the most potent talismanic patterns are the hand and fish. Here they are combined with sundiscs and cocks, themselves a solar symbol believed to drive away the evil spirits of the night.

145 Woman's jacket, Le Kef, Tunisia. The fish, an ancient phallic symbol, is a major amulet in Tunisian life. It features on embroideries, usually together with the hand, hangs from rearview mirrors of taxis and is painted over thresholds and at the bottom of soup bowls.

146 Woman's cap, Chitral, northern Pakistan. Materials added to embroidery increase its potency against evil spirits. One of the most widely appreciated, as it resembles the female vulva, is the cowrie. On this cap an old coke bottle top, buttons, the tree of life and red further enhance protection.

147 Below: Man's robe, Ethiopia. Metal discs and pendants are sewn over the ears and back neck of this robe and decorate the edges, which have appliquéd triangles of fabric as additional ornamentation.

148 Right: Child's jacket, Kohistan, northern Pakistan. Coins, believed to heal and avert evil, were often replaced by buttons. Old zips form an effective metallic edging.

149 Woman's cap, Yemen. Blue beads are associated with the power of the evil eye and one is sufficient to protect the wearer.

150 Child's jacket, Rajput caste, Kutch, India. Mirror was believed to dazzle the evil eye and even blind it. Just one, strategically placed at the centre back waist, would ensure the child's safety.

151 Woman's face mask, Yemen. Sequins have much in common with mirror in their protective role. Here the combination of small triangles in brass chain and mother-of-pearl, and the colour red, increases their power.

152 Pouch, Plains Indians, North America. Fringes and tassels – and in this case feathers – around the edge of an embroidery were already a feature of the Pazyryk textiles. Their movement distracts and confuses evil spirits and they are a ubiquitous device on textiles.

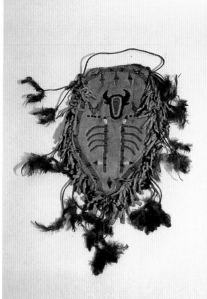

THE POWER OF RED

153 Ritual cloth, Naga, N.E. India. This cloth could only be worn by a man whose father and grandfather, and he himself, had sacrificed mithan buffalo and completed the whole cycle of necessary ceremonies. Red dog's hair, cowries, stripes and patterns on Naga textiles all had ritual meaning.

154 Man's cap, Sierra Leone. Symbolic motifs of crosses over arches and a lizard are embroidered on this cap which has a small, powerful piece of red applique at the forehead and nape.

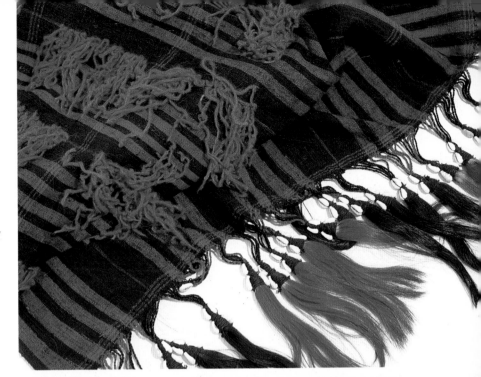

155 Woman's hood, Micmac Indian, North America. Red is the most powerful and vibrant of colours, associated with blood and thus with life and death. It is often used protectively in the form of appliquéd red fabric.

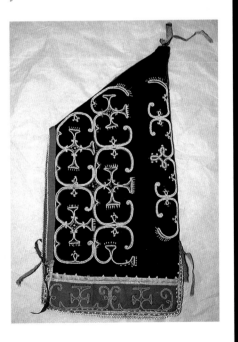

156 Left: *Woman's bag, Sweden. The peasant tradition of Europe associates red particularly with young women and with marriage. It is the dominant colour in all costume.*

157 Above: *Fertility doll, Ghana. The relationship of red to blood and fertility is expressed in the simple red cord of this doll, used by a woman when she wants a child.*

158 *Sampler, Italy. Trousseau linens are often also numbered in red cross stitch as laundry was a communal activity. The marking and repairing of linen was the motivation for the red alphabet and plain sewing samplers of the schoolgirls of Europe.*

159 *Trousseau aprons, France. The linen of Western Europe is marked in red cross stitch, reflecting primitive man's marking of objects in blood. This pile of aprons, made by 'DJ' for her trousseau, remains neatly folded and unused as her hand was never sought in marriage.*

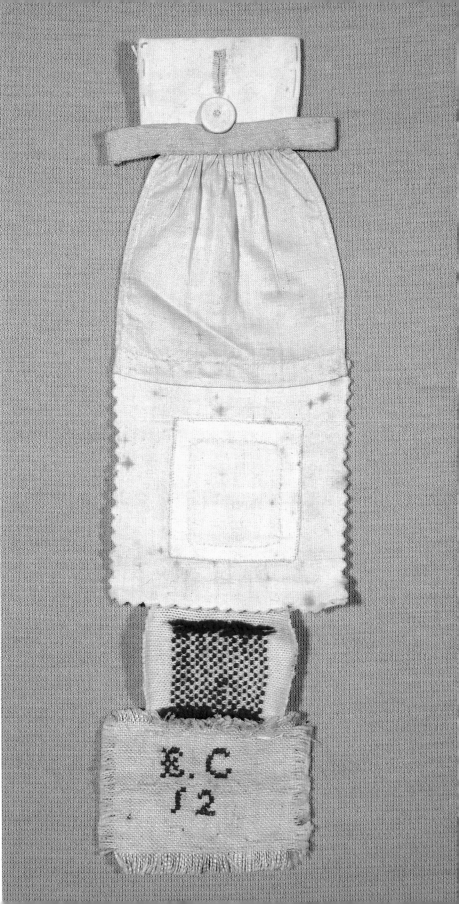

160   Bedcurtain, kutnice, Moravia. The curtain protecting mother and newborn child depicted the tulip, pomegranate and carnation of fertility; the stag and heart of hunting mythology; or the Christian IHS.

161   Marriage undershift, El Jem, Tunisia. In many countries, after consummation of the marriage the embroidered shift with its blood stains was shown by the bride's mother to the village women to prove her daughter's virginity.

162   Betel bag, Banjara caste, India. The exchange of embroidered gifts is part of marriage ritual. Brides of the nomadic Banjara traditionally worked a betel bag for their groom. In Europe the gift was usually a linen shirt.

163 Right: *Tab, probably from skirt hem, Paracas, Peru. Textiles of the Paracas mummy bundles, dating from 400 to 250 BC, included embroideries depicting trophy heads, part of the mythology concerned with the role of death in sustaining life.*

164 Below: *Woman's sarong,* lau hada, *Sumba, Indonesia. Crustaceans and lizards are symbols of rebirth. Sarongs were part of the dowry and were also grave gifts. Sumba chiefs were required to bury hundreds of textiles with their dead.*

165 *Shawl, Manipur, N.E. India. The Naga erected monolithic stones in honour of their dead. When a man had arranged this Herculean task, had offered feasting to his people and had lived apart from his family for one year, he was entitled to wear a shawl embroidered with animals.*

HOLY PLACES

166   Cloth, Cičmany, Slovakia. The holy corner of palaeolithic hunting societies, and of those who worshipped the earth goddess and placed figurines of her at their hearth, lingers in the holy corner of the European home. Embroidered cloths are hung over a triangular shelf with religious momentoes or over a picture of Madonna and child. This hub of the home is by the stove or in the corner of the room by the family table.

167   Cloth, Banske Bystrica, Slovakia. The icons and religious pictures of the ancient holy corner have in the modern world gradually been replaced by records of family rites of passage; wedding photos, certificates of military service and the television set. They are still draped with an embroidered cloth.

168   Cloth, bostani, Bengal. Embroidered cloths, kanthas, wrapped and protected precious objects. Making them was a ritual activity and the motifs chosen were symbolic: the central lotus, a tree of life in each corner, solar whorls and a gateway. Small objects from the women's daily lives – earrings, mirror, comb, betel cutters - fill the spaces.

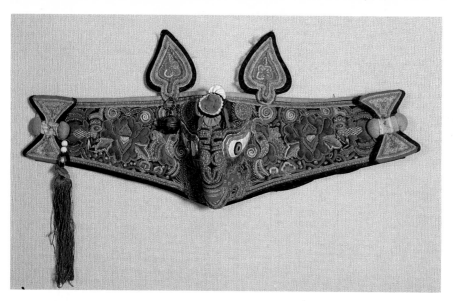

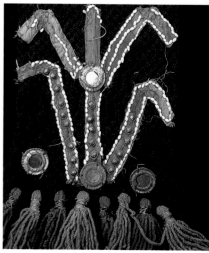

169 Child's headband, S.W. China. Children are the most precious of all objects to be protected by embroidery. In China boys (but not girls, who are considered unimportant) are dressed in hats embroidered with animal faces to fool evil spirits. To the horned bull are added other protective devices: bells, beads, tassels and pieces of red fabric.

170 Spoon bag, Baluch, Pakistan. For the nomadic Baluch, among their valuable possessions to be protected by embroidery are their spoons. Mirrors in metal surrounds, tassels and a tree of life, reminiscent of horn patterns and applied with cowries, will deter passing evil spirits.

171 Bullock's horn cover, Lammani caste, India. Animals were protected from harm by being branded with magical symbols and hung with amulets. For special occasions they were decorated with embroidered regalia increasing that protection and also displaying their owner's wealth. Cowries and mirror were favoured talismanic additions.

The Ch'ing Miao of southern China are among the many peoples who carry their babies in embroidered cloths. Many boys also wear hats that are hung with talismanic devices or that disguise the child as an animal so that evil spirits will leave him alone.

Almost every society embroiders bags for money in the form of purses or hanging pockets. These are worked in the different styles and techniques of each people but, unless subjected to commerce and fashion, always include protective motifs and materials.

Babies are, of course, among the most precious of all possessions and everywhere cradles are decorated with amulets and talismanic embroidery, almost always with something red. In the Russian territory of Dagestan on the Caspian Sea babies are still swaddled and covered with red. Children of south-west China are dressed in hats with animal faces to fool evil spirits, and wear night and day jerkins with highly decorated fronts, while in South-East Asia babies are toted around in richly embroidered carriers with tassels, pompoms and patterns of red.

Animals, too, are protected by amulets, by branding with symbols, and by embroidered regalia. Horses as animals of combat were protected physically by quilted covers, and in medieval Europe the decoration on their trappings and the rider's banner and shield served as identification at any passage of arms. The regalia of animals also displayed the owner's wealth and still sometimes in India and the Middle East on ceremonial occasions, particularly marriage, the domestic beasts of the family will be decked out in embroidered accoutrements: for bullocks horn covers, headdresses and hump cloths with rag birds; for camels, donkeys and horses' saddle covers, necklaces, kneebands and headcloths worked in the local style of embroidery or weaving. The Indian bridegroom traditionally arrived on a painted and caparisoned elephant and maharajahs rode in ceremonial processions swaying on howdahs strapped to elephants that shimmered with gold and silver embroidery, sequins, mirrors and rock crystal. The cars of today often betray the heritage of the past by the embroidered and sequined fish or triangle – or Saint Christopher – dangling from the rear view mirror.

Conclusion

The aesthetic beauty of embroidery made by the poorest of people stems from its inherent truth – truth of purpose, truth of material. Once this has gone – once the social context no longer exists and the beliefs and fears that embroidery promoted or deflected no longer torment, once linen is no longer painfully cultivated, spun and woven, sheep are no longer the mainstay of life and exotic silks from other lands a precious luxury – then traditional embroidery is doomed. It has become commercial: the tourist is an undiscerning purchaser, the trader accepts the crude and gaudy.

Slowly since the Industrial Revolution, gradually since the First World War and precipitately since the Second, technology, communications, changed values and lifestyles have disrupted all but a few pockets of human society. Even politics have played a role: the Communist rulers of Hungary with some pride replaced the old family marriage with mass weddings – 'splendid festivities at which the entire community happily participates, with the factory, plant and city workers who have given unselfish assistance throughout the year to the village in question being invited as guests'. It is hard to imagine the bride embroidering the traditional fine white handkerchief for them all. Nor, with the defeat of Communism and the return to Nationalism, are the old customs likely to be revived.

In embroidery the greatest motivation for change has been the education of girls: the Turkish girl can no longer only assure her future by embroidering exquisitely to gain a husband but is better equipped with perhaps a degree in civil engineering. Hope even glimmers for nomadic women such as the Baluch who lead a life of drudgery – erecting and dismantling tents, grinding corn, hauling water, cooking, raising children, weaving, embroidering and making carpets and felts, while their men tend the horses.

Attempts to revive traditional work by copying old patterns – by schools of embroidery, as in Istanbul and Salamanca, for example – are bound to fail when the social infrastructure has gone. The future lies with the individual embroideries of the West and possibly with those which have new-found social purpose such as the embroidered dresses of Palestinian women, worn throughout the Middle East as a political statement of affiliation to the Palestinian cause.

The ritual and social purpose of peasant and tribal embroidery, the symbolism of motifs that have lingered from the prehistoric era, are doomed to disappear within our lifetime. Clearly, it is already too late to be certain of the meaning and origin of many patterns and the purpose of much embellishment, but the juxtaposition of archaic embroideries from many parts of the world highlights a common theme: faith in the power of decoration to tame the gods and control the destiny of man.

Bibliography

General

Comte Goblet d'Alviella, *La Migration des Symboles*, Paris 1892

Robert Brain, *The Decorated Body*, London 1979

M.E. Burkett, *The Art of the Felt Maker*, Kendal 1979

Joseph Campbell, *Primitive Mythology: The Masks of God*, London 1976

Pamela Clabburn, *The Needleworker's Dictionary*, New York 1976

J.C. Cooper, *An Illustrated Encyclopaedia of Traditional Symbols*, London 1978

Jane P. Dwyer, *The Chronology and Iconography of Paracas-Style Textiles*, The Junius B. Bird Pre-Columbian Textile Conference, Washington 1973

Mincea Eliade, *Patterns in Comparative Religion*, London 1958

Sir James Frazer, *The Golden Bough*, London 1963

Marija Gimbutas, *Ancient Symbolism in Lithuanian Folk Art*, Philadelphia 1958

Macide Gönül, *Turkish Embroideries XV1–XIX Centuries*, Istanbul n.d.

Jean-Paul Lebeuf, *Broderie et Symbolisme chez les Kanouri et les Kotoko*, in *Objets et Mondes*, vol.IV, Paris 1970

Benjamin Pereira, *Têxteis: Tecnologia e simbolismo*, Lisbon 1985

Herta Puls, *Textiles of the Kuna Indians*, Princes Risborough 1988

Tamara Talbot Rice, *The Scythians*, London 1957

Tamara Talbot Rice, *Ancient Arts of Central Asia*, London 1965

Sergei Rudenko, trans. M.W. Thompson, *Frozen Tombs of Siberia*, London 1970

Mary Thomas, *Dictionary of Embroidery Stitches*, London 1934

The Great Goddess

Georges Charrière, *L'Art Barbare Scythe*, Paris 1971

Marija Gimbutas, *The Goddesses and Gods of Old Europe: Myths and Cult Images*, 1982

Marija Gimbutas, *The Language of the Goddess*, London 1990

François Hébert-Stevens, *L'Art Ancien de l'Amérique du Sud*, Paris 1972

Tamás Hofer and Edit Fél, *Hungarian Folk Art*, Budapest 1975, Oxford 1979

E.O. James, *The Cult of the Mother Goddess*, London 1961

Vassos Karageorghis, *Cypriote Antiquities in the Pierides Collection*, Lanarca, Cyprus n.d.

Gyula László, *L'Art des Nomades*, Paris 1972

Museum of Mankind, *Turkish Folk Embroideries*, London 1981

Erich Neumann, *The Great Mother*, London 1955

Merrell Oliver, *Goddesses and Their Offspring: 19th- and 20th-century Eastern European Embroideries*, Binghamton N.Y. 1986

Eduardo Herrán Gómez de la Torre, *The Nasca Lines: New designs, new enigmas*, Lima 1985

The Tree of Life

Roger Cook, *The Tree of Life: Symbol of the Centre*, London 1974

H. Danthine, *Le Palmier-dattier et les arbres sacrés dans l'iconographie de l'Asie occidentale ancienne*, Paris 1937

Nell Parrott, *Les représentations de l'arbre sacré sur les monuments de Mésopotamie et d'Elam*, Paris 1937

Stephen J. Reno, *The Sacred Tree as an Early Christian Literary Symbol*, Saarbrücken 1978

The Hunt

Muriel Baker and Margaret Lunt, *Blue & White: The Cotton Embroideries of Rural China*, New York 1977

Ljiljara Beljkasic-Hadzidedic, *The Folk Art of Bosnia & Hercegovina*, Sarajevo 1983

Laurence Delaby, *Figurations sibériennes d'oiseaux à usage religieux*, in *Objets et Mondes*, vol.III, Paris 1970

Krystyna Deuss, *Indian Costumes from Guatemala*, Manchester 1981

Arnold van Gennep, *Les Rites de Passage*, Paris 1908

Glenbow-Alberta Institute, *The Spirit Sings: Artistic Traditions of Canada's First Peoples*, Toronto 1987

S. Giedion, *The Eternal Present: The Beginnings of Art*, Oxford 1962

Joan Halifax, *Shaman: The Wounded Healer*, London 1982

Carl Hentze, *Mythes et Symboles Lunaires*, Antwerp 1932

T.C. Hodson, *The Naga Tribes of Manipur*, London 1911

J.C.H. King, *Thunderbird and Lightning*, London 1982

G.S. Maslova, *Motifs from Russian Folk Embroidery*, Moscow 1978

E.D. Phillips, *The Royal Hordes: Nomad Peoples of the Steppes*, London 1965

Carl Schuster, *Some Peasant Embroideries from Western China*, in *Embroidery*, vol.III, no. 4, 1935

Geoffrey Turner, *Hair Embroidery in Siberia & North America*, Oxford 1976

The Sun
Ethel-Jane W. Bunting, *Sindhi Tombs & Textiles: The Persistence of Pattern*, Alburquerque 1980
René-Yves Creston, *Le Costume Breton*, Paris 1974
Walter Herdeg (ed.), *The Sun in Art*, Zürich 1962
Paulina Mitreva, *Embroideries from Samokov*, Sofia 1982
Olga Ostric, *Motiv 'cetvorokuke' na vezenojcohi u narodnoj Nosnji Zadarskog podrucia*, Zadar 1972

Religion and its Patterns
Térésa Battesti, *Signification sociale du vêtement Zoroastrien féminin*, in L'Ethnographie, Vêtement et Sociétés, Paris 1979
Dominique Champault and A.R. Verbrugge, *La Main: ses figurations au Maghreb et au Levant*, Paris 1965
Dominique Champault, *L'Izar de Qaracoche*, in Objets et Mondes, vol.IX, Fasc. 2, Paris 1969
Vickie C. Elson, *Dowries from Kutch*, Los Angeles 1971
Emel Esin, *Sa'dullah Pasa Yalisi*, Istanbul 1977
John Irwin and Margaret Hall, *Indian Embroidery*, Ahmedabad 1972
Karl Jettmar and Volker Thewalt, *Between Gandhara and the Silk Roads*, Oxford 1987
Julia Nicholson, *Traditional Indian Arts of Gujarat*, Leicester 1988
Jessica Rawson, *Chinese Ornament: The Lotus & the Dragon*, London 1984
David Talbot Rice, *Islamic Art*, London 1975
Ninian Smart, *The World's Religions*, Cambridge 1989
Victoria and Albert Museum, *The Indian Heritage: Court Life & Arts Under Mughal Rule*, 1982
John Vollmer, *In the Presence of the Dragon Throne*, Toronto 1977
Wang Yarong, *Chinese Folk Embroidery*, London 1987

Evil Spirits
Ibn Battúta, *Travels in Asia & Africa 1325–1354*, London 1929
Roloff Beny and Sylvia A. Matheson, *Symbolism: Rajasthan*, London n.d.
Jeanne Biby-Brossard, *Les Broderies Rustiques au XIXe siècle* in Soc. Hist. et Sc. des Deux-Sèvres, vol.III, 1970
Cincius V.I., *Les représentations des Neghidales liées à la chasse*, Leningrad 1971
Yves Delaporte, *Communication et Signification dans les Costumes Populaires*, Paris 1979
V. Diószegi (ed.), *Popular Beliefs & Folklore Tradition in Siberia*, Budapest 1968
M.E. Durham, *Some Tribal Origins, Laws & Customs of the Balkans*, London 1928
Dr Otto Finsch, *Uber Bekleidung, Schmuck und Tätowirung der Papuas der Südostküste von Neu-Guinea*, Vienna 1885
Beni Gupta, *Magical Beliefs & Superstitions*, Delhi 1979
W.L. Hildburgh, *Some Japanese Minor Magical or Religious Practices Connected with Travelling*, London 1916
Bernhard Karlgren, *Some Fecundity Symbols in Ancient China*, Stockholm 1930
Astrid and Joachim Knuf, *Amulette und Talismane: Symbole des magischen Alltags*, Cologne 1984

Mária Kresz, *The Art of the Hungarian Furriers*, Budapest 1979
Avril Lansdell, *The Clothes of the Cut*, British Waterways Board, London n.d.
Ildikó Lehtinen, *Naisten Korut (Women's jewellery in Central Russia and Western Siberia)*, Helsinki 1979
Paul and Elaine Lewis, *Peoples of the Golden Triangle*, London & N.Y. 1984
Dr S. Mahdihassan and Dr M. Gerhardt, *The Evil Eye: Its Defeat in Oriental Art*, Hoechst News 54, Frankfurt 1971
Brigitte Menzel, *Textilien aus Westafrika II*, Berlin 1972
Musée des Arts et Traditions Populaires, *Costume-Coutume*, Paris 1987
Edmond O'Donovan, *The Merv Oasis*, London 1882
Anne Paul, *The Symbolism of Paracas Turbans: a Consideration of Style, Serpents & Hair*, in Nawpa Pacha, vol.20, Berkeley 1982
Nikola Pentelio, *The Origin & Symbolism of Embellishment & Jewellery*, Belgrade 1971
John Picton and John Mack, *African Textiles*, London 1979
Denise Pop-Câmpeanu, *Se Vêtir: Quand, pourquoi, comment en Roumanie hier et aujourd'hui*, Freiburg 1984
Chloë Sayer, *Mexican Costume*, London 1985
S. Seligmann, *Der Böse Blick und Verwandtes*, Berlin 1910
R.B. Serjeant and R. Lewcock, *Sana'a: An Arabic Islamic City*, London 1983
Caroline Stone, *The Embroideries of North Africa*, Harlow 1985
Anne Pike Tay and Robert Moes, *Mingei: Japanese Folk Art*, New York 1985
Shelagh Weir, *Palestinian Embroidery*, London 1970
Shelagh Weir, *Palestinian Costume*, London 1989
Popi Zora, *Embroideries & Jewellery of Greek National Costume*, Athens 1981

The Power of Red
Heide Nixdorff and Heidi Müller, *Weisse Westen, Rote Roben*, Berlin 1983
Penelope Walton, *Needlework from Jorvik*, in Embroidery, vol.36, no.4, 1985
Lubon K. Wolynetz, *Rushnyky: Ukrainian Ritual Cloths*, Binghamton, N.Y. 1986

High Days
Marie Jeanne Adams, *System & Meaning in East Sumba Textile Design: A Study in Traditional Indonesian Art*, New Haven 1969
R. Brunschwig, *La Berbérie Orientale sous les Hafsides des Origines à la Fin du XVs*, Tunis 1947
Raina Drazheva, *Paganistic Heritage in the Agrarian Rites of the Bulgarians*, Liverpool 1989
M. Gittinger, *Splendid Symbols: Textiles & Traditions in Indonesia*, Washington 1979
Jean Guiart (ed.), *Rites de la Mort*, Paris 1979
Robert J. Holmgren and Anita E. Spertus, *Early Indonesian Textiles from Three Island Cultures*, New York 1989
Jeanne Jouin, *Le Vêtement Mis à l'Envers*, in l'Ethnographie, Vêtement et Sociétés 2, Paris 1984

Marika Diener-Kovács, *Les Conséquences d'une Loi Somptuaire sur le Vêtement des Matyó*, in *l'Ethnographie, Vêtement et Sociétés 2*, Paris 1984

Brigitte Khan Majuis, *Indonesische Textilien: Wege zu Göttern und Ahnen*, Cologne 1984

Ganka Mihailova, *The traditional Bulgarian costume as a reflection of folk notions about the world, nature and man*, Liverpool 1989

Marie-Louise Nabholz-Kartaschoff and Marlène Lang-Mayer, *Götter, Tiere, Blumen*, Basle 1987

Gertrud Grenander Nyberg, *Lanthemmens Prydnadssöm*, Stockholm 1983

M. Stehlíková, *L'Udové Zdobené Plachty*, Martin, Czechoslovakia 1966

Mildred Stapley, *Popular Weaving and Embroidery in Spain*, Madrid 1924

Martha and Catherine Wilmot, *The Russian Journals*, London 1934

Holy Places

Moira Broadbent, *Animal Regalia*, Whitchurch 1985

Johannes de Plano Carpini, *Voyage into the North East Part of the World, in the Year of Our Lord 1246*, Haklyt Society, London 1900

Alfred Janata and Nassim Jawad, *Ein Aspekt religiöser Volkskunst der Hazara*, Bibliotheca Afghanica, Liestal 1983

Zaman Niaz, *The Art of Kantha Embroidery*, Dacca 1981

Mohammed Sayeedur Rahman, *The Common Ground*, in *Woven Air*, London 1988

Friar William of Rubruck, *The Journey of William of Rubruck*, trans. & ed. W.W. Rockhill, Haklyt Society, London 1900

Kathryn Salomon, *Jewish Ceremonial Embroidery*, London 1988

Gertrud Weinhold, *Zeit und Raum zur Ehre Gottes*, Berlin 1984

Collections and Collecting

Karen Finch and Greta Putnam, *Caring for Textiles*, London 1977

Cecil Lubell, *Textile Collections of the World*, vol.1 United States, Canada, London 1976, vol.2 United Kingdom & Ireland, London 1976, vol.3 France, London 1978

Quotation on p.7 taken from J. Newall, in *The Embroideress*, vol.I, 1924

Collections and Collecting

Collections

Collections of peasant and tribal embroidery are mainly to be found in ethnology, folk and local museums rather than in major museums of textile history or of decorative arts. A handful of individual museums are world famous for their collections, which include such material. They are:

Victoria and Albert Museum, London
Royal Scottish Museum, Edinburgh
Royal Ontario Museum, Toronto

Ethnology and Archaeology Museums holding international collections of which embroideries are a part (particular specialities are bracketed):

Musée de l'Homme, Paris (Yugoslavian, Siberian, Arab)
Museum für Völkerkunde, Vienna
Museum für Völkerkunde, Basle
Museum für Völkerkunde, Zürich
Museum für Völkerkunde, Berlin
Rautenstrauch-Joest Museum für Völkerkunde, Cologne
Museum of Mankind, London (Palestinian)
Pitt-Rivers Museum, Oxford (hair embroidery, Naga)
University Museum of Archaeology & Ethnology, Cambridge, England (Paracas)
Musée des Arts Africains et Océaniens, Paris (Maghreb)
Smithsonian National Museum of Natural History, Washington
Peabody Museum of Archeology & Ethnology, Cambridge, Mass.
Field Museum of Natural History, Chicago (Chinese peasant)
Museum of Natural History, Newark (Tibetan)
Museum of New Mexico, Santa Fé (Palestinian)
Horniman Museum, London

Ethnology Museums holding national, regional or ethnic collections:

Museum of the American Indian, New York
Museu de Etnologia, Lisbon
Ethnology Museum, Moscow
Ethnology Museum, Leningrad
Ethnology Museum, Martin (Slovakian)
Ethnology Museum, Brno (Moravian)
Ethnology Museum, Ljubljana (Slovene)
Ethnology Museum, Zagreb (Croatian)

National Museums with significant embroidery collections:

Benaki Museum, Athens
Finnish National Museum, Helsinki
Hungarian National Museum, Budapest
Bulgarian National Museum, Sofia
Yugoslav National Museum, Belgrade
Topkapi Museum, Istanbul

Israel Museum, Jerusalem
Yemen National Museum, Sana'a

Folk Museums, most holding the major collections for the countries concerned:

Deutsche Volkskunde, Berlin
Altonaer Museum, Hamburg
Arnhem Open Air Museum, Arnhem, Holland
Danish Folk Museum, Copenhagen
Nordic Museum, Stockholm
Norwegian Folk Museum, Oslo
Schweizerisches Landesmuseum, Zürich
Musée des Arts et Traditions Populaires, Paris
Museum of Greek Folk Art, Athens
Jordan Museum of Popular Traditions, Amman
Azem Palace Museum, Damascus

Art Museums whose collections include some peasant embroidery:

Hermitage Museum, Leningrad (Pazyryk material and Russian)
Metropolitan Museum, New York
Brooklyn Museum (Russian)
Boston Museum of Fine Arts (Greek Island and Oriental)
Cleveland Museum of Art
Indianapolis Museum of Art (Balkan and Moroccan)
Detroit Institute of Art (Czech)
Museu de Arte Antiga, Lisbon (Indo-Portuguese)
Fitzwilliam Museum, Cambridge (Middle Eastern)
Whitworth Art Gallery, Manchester (Mediterranean, Eastern European)
Ashmolean Museum, Oxford (Oriental)
Museum of History and Art, Zagorsk (Russian)
Museum of Cultural History, Los Angeles (Indian)
Instituto Valencia de Don Juan, Madrid (Spanish)

Museums of Historical Embroidery with some peasant work:

Museo Pedagógico Textil, Madrid
Museu Tèxtil i d'Indumentària, Barcelona
Calico Museum of Textiles, Ahmedabad

All major museums have more embroideries in reserve than on display and require appointments to show these. For the casual visitor local museums can be very rewarding as their collections are often easier to see. Particularly good are those in Eastern Europe, such as the regional ones of Yugoslavia as at Zadar, Sarajevo and Skopje, or those of Portugal, Tunisia and Morocco, where that of Tétouan is of special interest. In Turkey the ethnology museums of Bursa, Kayseri and Konya have embroideries, as does the Sadberk Hanim Museum of Buyukdere, which is a delight. In India the Shreyas Folk Museum of Ahmedabad features costume.

Most local museums cover local costumes but some will have a specialist embroidery collection, as do the Leicestershire Museum (Indian) and the Angoulême Museum in France (Moroccan). Often this will have been donated by a collector, as with part of the Wace collection of

Mediterranean and Near Eastern at the Merseyside museums of Liverpool, and the collection of Albanian and Yugoslavian embroideries at the Bankfield, Halifax, donated by the redoubtable Miss Durham – who first went out to Montenegro in 1900 and returned continuously to the Balkans until the First World War, giving medical assistance, collecting embroideries and, it is reported, separating squabbling Albanians with her umbrella.

Collecting

The collector has first to realize that embroideries that were an inherent part of social custom and served to identify the wearer were not originally made for sale. They thus appear on the market in a haphazard way. An exception is Chinese embroidery, for which there is a steady and consistent market.

Choice of collection should not be too specialized, as it will prove difficult to achieve a worthwhile grouping. It is best based on a region – say Eastern Europe or the Middle East – rather than being confined to perhaps Hungary or Syria. The basis of a collection could also be a particular technique such as tambouring or smocking, or stitch such as cross.

First a visit to relevant museums is essential so that the collector is aware of the quality and range that should be taken as guidelines. Most museums have far more in reserve than on display, and because of conservation problems appointments to view are not always easy to obtain.

The period at which costume was discarded affects its availability. Items abandoned soon after the First World War are more difficult to find than articles which have only recently been given up in favour of Western dress and may still be kept in cupboards and chests. Often there is great reluctance to sell something that has been in the family for generations and the collector should never bring pressure to bear. There is a growing awareness that historical embroideries belong to a vanishing heritage, and they have therefore become more precious to the society that created

them. For this reason they are often more expensive in the country of their origin.

Because of the fickleness of the market it is possible to find embroideries in the most bizarre of places – car boot sales, for instance, or flea markets – but for sustained collecting, textile auctions are the best source. Regular attendance also gives some idea of prices, though these can vary enormously for rather arbitrary reasons.

There are a few specialist dealers, some of whom own premises while others work directly with customers or by staging exhibitions. Some galleries and shops specialize in 'ethnic' articles and these will include embroideries. The textile world is close-knit and once a collection is embarked on, a snowball effect is soon discovered, with other collectors and dealers proving to be friendly and helpful.

Conservation of embroideries is of immense importance. If they are to be hung on walls the windows should be treated with protective film against ultraviolet light. Silk is particularly vulnerable to light and most colours fade. Items should not be folded as the fibres will eventually break at the fold, silk again being especially weak in this respect. Instead they should be rolled and protected by acid-free tissue. Cardboard rolls from packets of aluminium foil, or gleaned from fabric shops, are a useful base. Ideally, dresses should be laid flat rather than hung. Wool, of course, is susceptible to moth and creepy-crawlies, for whom also starch is a good meal. Woollen embroideries should therefore be aired frequently and cotton ones should not be left starched. No steps should ever be taken that are irreversible. Washing especially should hardly ever be attempted by the amateur.

The purpose of a collection may vary. It can be for the satisfaction of rescuing neglected embroideries, for the pleasure of enhancing one's home, as a source of inspiration for one's own embroidery or other craft where ideas of colour and design can be appropriated, or as a tool for teaching others. There is little point in amassing articles simply to keep them hidden away in cupboards and drawers, and their ultimate destination should always be borne in mind when buying.

Glossary

acanthus: foliage design based on the Mediterranean plant *Acanthus spinosus*, widely used in European arts

appliqué: needlework technique where pieces of fabric are sewn on to the ground material to make a design

arabesque: stylized interlaced foliage pattern which reached European arts from the Middle East in the sixteenth century

ashon: a *kantha* for guests to sit on at weddings

batik: technique of decorating textiles by the application of wax to retain undyed areas in the design

betel: leaf of the *Piper betle* which Indians chew together with lime and the nut of the *Areca catechu*

bey: a Turkish governor

boteh: curvilinear shape with curled top derived from Persian flower spray pattern and perfected during the Mughal period in India. Popularly associated with shawls.

bouclé: a yarn or fabric of bulky loops

brocading: the addition during weaving of supplementary weft threads to give a raised pattern

broderie anglaise: white cotton eyelet embroidery which developed in England in the mid-nineteenth century

caftan: long loose robe with full sleeves, worn especially in North Africa and the Middle East

caliph: ruler of Muslim empire

canvaswork: embroidery worked on evenweave canvas fabric by counting threads

couching: technique where a thread is laid on fabric and attached by stitching with another thread, usually finer

crêpe: crinkly fabric of tightly spun yarn

damask: fabric with woven design that is reversible, generally shiny to matt

drawn threadwork: openwork technique where threads are removed from the ground fabric

etamine: fine loosely woven fabric, usually cotton

eyelet: embroidery of holes strengthened by stitchery

fichu: large wraparound collar, usually of delicate fabric

filet: handmade net darned with like thread (*see also* lacis)

floss silk: very shiny untwisted raw silk

fulling: process for shrinking woven cloth and thus thickening it

gauze: very fine open fabric with twisted warp threads, usually silk

godet: triangular piece of fabric inserted into a garment for fullness

griffin: an imaginary creature with the body of a lion and the head and talons of an eagle

icon: in Orthodox religion a sacred painting or mosaic representing Christ or a saint

ikat: technique in which the warp threads, and occasionally both warp and weft, are dyed with the design of the fabric before weaving commences

kantha: traditional quilted cloth of Bengal

kit: embroidery with the design already prepared, supplied with instructions and the requisite threads

lacis: handmade net darned with like thread (*see also* filet)

lappet: long piece of fabric hanging from the side of a cap

menorah: seven branched candlestick of the Jewish liturgy associated, when stylized, with the tree of life

mihrab: arched niche in a mosque marking the direction of Mecca

needlepoint: in England lace made with a needle, in America canvaswork

paisley: *boteh* pattern commonly used on European shawls of the nineteenth century imitating Kashmiri ones, many of which were made in Paisley

palmette: stylized palm leaf of classical decoration

pattern books: books of designs for artisans, published from the early sixteenth century, mainly in Germany and Italy

portière: curtain hung around or over a doorway

pulledwork: openwork technique in which threads of the ground fabric are teased apart rather than withdrawn

purdah: Indian system of screening women from public gaze

purl: coiled hollow gold wire for embroidery

rath: a wheeled carriage transporting the idol of Vishnu

resist dye: technique where a dye-resistant paste is used to retain undyed areas in the design

runic: ancient Germanic alphabet

saz: Ottoman design of round stemless blossom encircled by curling leaf, named from 'reed pen' drawing

stele: standing stone, usually carved

stencil dye: technique where stencils are used to retain undyed areas in the design

stūpa: a Buddhist dome-shaped memorial shrine

tambouring: chain stitch worked with a hook instead of a needle

tie-dye: technique of tying small bunches in fabric before dyeing so that these areas remain undyed

wazir: Muslim minister of state

Sources of Illustrations

p.66: Venus of Lespugue, Musée de l'Homme, Paris.
Minoan figurine, British Museum GR 1864.2.2.0.32.
Perfume bottle, British Museum GR 1860.4.4.30.
Towel, Russia, private collection, Paris.
p.67: Detail from great felt, Pazyryk, Hermitage Museum, Leningrad.
Figurine, Historical Museum of Razgrad, Bulgaria.
p.68: François Hébert-Stevens.
p.69: Minoan seals, British Museum GR 1947 9–26.2, GR 1921 7–11.2.
Ritual mounted worshippers on peasant embroidery, Wang Yarong.
Terracotta horse and rider, Boetia, Greece, British Museum GR 1949 7–10.1.
Cover, Mithila, India, Calico Museum of Textiles, Ahmedabad, 99A.287.
Napkin, Turkey, Ethnographic Museum, Ankara.
p.70: Pomegranate motif, *suzani*, Nurata, author's collection.
Carnation motif, woman's coat, Aleppo, Syria, author's collection.
Carnation motif, Coptic cloth AC828, Musée du Louvre, Paris.

The Tree of Life

p.71: Gold jewelry, Crete, British Museum GR 1892.5–20.17.
Tcheremiss people in festive dress, National Board of Antiquities, Helsinki, Finland.
p.72: Woman's dress, Qutayfé, Syria, Azem Palace Museum, Damascus.
Calcutta, author's photograph.
Burial shift from Martovce, Tamás Hofer, Edit Fél.
p.73: Paulina Mitreva.

The Hunt

p.74: Author's collection.
p.75: Saddle lining, *shabrack*, Pazyryk, Hermitage Museum. Rudenko.
Mantle, Kunsthistorisches Museum, Weltlicher Schatzkammer, Vienna, X111 14.
Sleeve, woman's blouse, Salamanca. Museum of Decorative Arts, Madrid.
Valance, from the Carl Schuster collection, Field Museum of Natural History, Chicago, FM 234389.
p.76: Gold bovine plaque, Historical Museum of Varna, Bulgaria.
Photograph, Čičmany, c.1906. Slovak National Ethnographic Museum 135060.
Headscarf, G.S. Maslova.
p.77: Pot, Kansu and ritual bronze, China. Carl Hentze.
Man's slipper-sock, Bosansko Grahovo, Zemaljski Museum of Bosnia-Herzegovina, Sarajevo, Yugoslavia.
p.78: Sassanid and Egyptian headgear, Slovakian hair arrangements, after drawings by Ursula Müller in Heide Nixdorff exhibition 'Festive Folk Costume', leaflet 3, Berlin 1977, Staatliche Museen Preussischer Kulturbesitz Berlin, Museum für Völkerkunde, Abt. Europa.
Uygur woman, cave painting, Chotsko, Turfan, China.

Stone idol, Minoussinsk, Carl Hentze.
p.79: Salmon-skin marriage robe, Ghiliak, Musée de l'Homme, Paris 62.11.1.
p.80: Russian altar frontal, Historical Museum, Moscow, 15494. R.B.-1.

The Sun

p.80: Solar pictographs, Walter Herdeg.
Bouriate drawing, Carl Hentze.
p.106: Photograph Peter Stradling, Devon.
p.107: Woman's jacket, Pont l'Abbé, Brittany. Musée de Bretagne, Rennes D.60.48/51.
Serbian woman's jacket, Olga Ostric.
p.108: Rudenko.
p.109: Karl Jettmar, Volker Thewalt.
p.110: Ethel-Jane W. Bunting.

3 Religion and its Patterns

p.111: Hanging, Hong Kong, author's collection.
p.113: Jessica Rawson.
p.114: Wolfram Eberhard, *Lexikon chinesischer Symbole*, Cologne 1983.
p.115: Turban cover, cushion cover, cloth, Topkapi Museum, Istanbul. Nurhayat Berker, *Islemeler*, Istanbul 1981.
Celestial kiosk, Dr Emil Esin.
p.116: Bath towel, napkin 31/1389, Topkapi Museum, Istanbul.
p.119: Goldwork bolero, Tunisia, author's collection.
Door, Benares, India, author's photograph.
p.129: Denise Pop-Câmpeanu.
p.130: Musée de l'Homme, Paris 67.100.77.

4 The Magical Source of Protection

p.131: Woman in Poprad, Slovak National Ethnographic Museum 17930.
p.134: Topkapi Museum, Istanbul 13/829.
p.135: Married woman's stomacher, Regional Museum of Pilsen, Bohemia.
Motif 'guardian of the breasts', Narodnoe Iskusstvo, *Il'mikra Medzitova: Marijskoe, Izzatel'stvo 1985*.
Tchuvash woman's dress, Musée de l'Homme, Paris 46.6.16.
p.136: National Board of Antiquities, Helsinki.
p.138: Čičmany, Slovakia, c.1950, private collection.
Terracotta figurine, Kara-tépé, Turkestan, Hermitage Museum, Leningrad; Copyright Editions Cercle d'Art, L'Art Barbare Scythe.
Russian statuette, Mária Kresz.
p.140: Musée National des Arts Africains et Océaniens, Paris MN.AM.1972.7.17.
p.141: Musées des Antiquités Nationales, St. Germain-en-Laye, France.
p.151: Linen drying, Zuberec, Slovakia, author's photograph.
p.152: Slovak National Ethnographic Museum 46255.
Cloth to prepare child for baptism, Daniel Baud-Bovy, *Peasant Art in Switzerland*, Studio 1924.

p.153: Linen cupboard, photograph Velke Krtiš, Slovak National Ethnographic Museum XIV-3107.

p.154: Author's collection.

p.157: Slovak National Ethnographic Museum 14895.

p.158: Author's collection.

p.159: Chimanlals, *Rangoli: Floor Patterns Book*, Bombay n.d.

p.160: Author's photograph.

p.177: Ch'ing Miao girls, near Anshun, Kweichow, South China. Photo Carl Schuster 1935. Archives of the Museum of Ethnography, Basle.

All line drawings are by Imogen Paine.

Acknowledgments

The task of naming individually all those who have contributed in one way or another to this book would be impossible, but the author no less warmly thanks everyone who has been involved in its creation.

The past fifteen years have been devoted to searching for the roots of embroidery and attempting to record the old traditions before they vanish for ever. A lone traveller, the author has been invited into the homes of women in many countries. She has sat on mud floors being offered ill-afforded dry bread and hot tea, or has scooped out food with her hands from a large bowl shared with the women and children after the men had had their fill and left. Such hospitality and insight into women's lives so freely given have been invaluable.

The staff of museums and libraries in many countries have been unstinting in their help and interest and, as a professional linguist and master of five languages, the author has also been able to consult foreign sources, both published and in archives.

To all, from ethnographers of world repute to the simple village women who so painstakingly described their lives, the author extends her most grateful thanks.

Index

Main references are indicated in **bold** type. Numerals in *italic* refer to the colour illustration numbers; black-and-white photographs and line drawings are listed last, by page number, in roman type.